BEDROOM FARCE

First produced at the Library Theatre, Scarborough in June, 1975 and subsequently at the National Theatre, London in March 1977 with the following cast of characters:

Ernest	Michael Gough
Delia	Joan Hickson
Nick	Michael Kitchen
Jan	Polly Adams
Malcolm	Derek Newark
Kate	Susan Littler
Trevor	Stephen Moore
Susannah	Maria Atken

The play directed by Alan Ayckbourn and Peter Hall
Setting by Timothy O'Brien and Tazeena Firth

The action takes place in three bedrooms

Act I   Saturday evening, 7 pm
Act II   A few moments later

Time—the present

BEDROOM
FARCE
A Comedy

ALAN AYCKBOURN

SAMUEL  FRENCH

LONDON
NEW YORK TORONTO SYDNEY HOLLYWOOD

ACT I

Three bedrooms. Saturday evening, 7 p.m.

The first bedroom is Ernest and Delia's. It is large and Victorian, in need of re-decoration. The furniture, including a double bed, bedside tables, dressing-table, etc., are all sturdy, unremarkable family pieces. There is a phone by the bed. A door leads to the landing and the rest of the house, another to a bathroom

The second bedroom is Malcolm and Kate's. This is smaller, probably a front bedroom in a terrace house which they are in the process of converting. It is sparsely furnished, a brand new bed, unmade, being the centrepiece. There is in addition a small stepladder. One of the walls has been re-papered, the rest are stripped. In one corner is a cardboard package, unopened. There is a phone by the bed. One door leads to the landing, and the rest of the house

The third bedroom is Nick and Jan's. This is furnished in a more trendy style, with a brass bedstead and some interesting antique stuff. There are rugs on the floor and a phone by the bed. A single door leads off to the bathroom and every-where else

When the CURTAIN *rises, Nick is already in bed, lying looking sorry for himself. Malcolm and Kate's room is empty*

Delia is sitting in her bedroom at her dressing-table mirror. She is going out. She is in her slip and finishing her make-up: an elaborate operation. Ernest wanders in. He is bird-like, bumbling, nearly sixty. He is in evening dress. He stares at Delia. They are obviously going to be late, but Ernest has learnt that impatience gets him nowhere

Ernest Have you got much further to go?
Delia (*without turning*) Not long now.
Ernest Good. Good show. (*He walks about humming restlessly*) No, that is definitely a damp patch, you know.
Delia Mmm?
Ernest A damp patch. Definitely. It's getting in from somewhere. I've just been standing on the spare bed in there feeling the ceiling. The verdict is, very, very damp. (*He goes to the window*)
Delia Oh dear.
Ernest (*opening the window*) Yes. Which only goes to confirm my suspicion that those chaps we had crawling about the roof for six months didn't know their job. (*He leans out of the window backwards*)
Delia What are you doing?
Ernest I'm trying to catch a glimpse of the re-pointing. It's seeping in from somewhere.

Delia You'll fall out in a minute.

Ernest No. You can't see a thing. That gutterwork's obscuring the whole ... Good Lord. That needs a spot of attention. It's hanging off at one end. Good Lord.

Delia Darling, you're in my light.

Ernest (*moving back inside*) There's a whole chunk of guttering here hanging on by a screw. Hadn't noticed that before. (*He shuts the window*)

Delia Oh, did I tell you. Susannah phoned this afternoon.

Ernest (*thoughtfully*) Did he? Did he indeed.

Delia No, not he. Susannah.

Ernest *Who?*

Delia Susannah.

Ernest Oh, Susannah. Jolly good. Very worrying that guttering, you know. One light to medium monsoon, we'll have a water-fall in the dining-room.

Delia She sounded very agitated.

Ernest Oh yes.

Delia Things are not good between her and Trevor.

Ernest Ah. (*He looks at his watch*) It's twenty past, you know.

Delia All right, all right.

Ernest We're booked for eight o'clock.

Delia They'll hold the table.

Ernest They might not.

Delia Of course they will.

Ernest You never know. Not these days.

Delia They'll hold the table for us. We're regulars. We go there every year.

Ernest Oh, well. It's your anniversary.

Delia And yours.

Ernest True, true. I think I should have given these shoes another polish.

Delia Well, go and do it.

Ernest No, it doesn't matter. Nobody'll notice.

Delia It would appear that things between Susannah and Trevor are coming to a head.

Ernest Ah.

Delia He was always a difficult boy. I sometimes think if you hadn't ignored him quite as much ...

Ernest I did?

Delia Of course you did. You hardly said a word to him all the time he was growing up.

Ernest I seem to remember chatting away to him for hours.

Delia Well. Chatting. I meant conversation. Conversation about important things. A father should converse with his son. About things that matter deeply.

Ernest Doesn't really leave them much to talk about then, does it?

Delia And that if I may say so is typical. No. Let's admit it. We weren't good parents. You did nothing and I tried to make up for it, and that's why he's like he is today. I mean if he'd had a stable childhood, he'd never have completely lost his sense of proportion and married Susannah. I mean, I sometimes feel on the rare occasions one does see them together that she's not really—awful thing to say but—not really resilient enough for Trevor. He wants somebody more phlegmatic. That Jan girl for instance would have been ideal. Do you remember her?

Ernest Jan? Jan? Jan?

Delia Nice little thing. Beautifully normal. She came to tea, do you remember? You got on very well with her.

Ernest Oh yes. She was very jolly, wasn't she? She was very interested in my stamps. What happened to her?

Delia Oh, she married—someone else, I think. She still writes occasionally.

Ernest I must say I preferred her to Susannah. Never really hit it off with her, I'm afraid.

Delia Well, she's a very complex sort of girl, isn't she? Hasn't really made up her mind. About herself. I mean, I think a woman sooner or later has simply got to make up her mind about herself. I mean, even if she's someone like Carolyn—you know, Mrs Brightman's Carolyn—who looks at herself and says, right, I'm a lump I'm going to be a lump but then at least everyone can accept her as a lump. So much simpler.

Ernest I think he should have married this other one.

Delia Jan? I don't think she was that keen.

Ernest She was altogether much jollier.

Delia Well, we're saddled with Susannah as a daughter-in-law—at least temporarily. We'd better make the best of it—I think I've put these eyes on crooked—we'd better make the best of it.

Ernest It's their bed. They can lie on it.

Delia Yes. I think that's one of the problems.

Ernest Eh?

Delia B–E–D.

Ernest B–E–D? Bed?

Delia Enough said.

Ernest Good Lord. How do you know?

Delia One reads between the lines, darling. I've had a little look around their house. You can tell a great deal from people's bedrooms.

Ernest Can you? Good heavens. (*He looks about*)

Delia If you know what to look for. Now then. (*She rises*) Do I wear what I wore when I went to the Reynolds or shall I wear the stripe thing that you loathe.

Ernest I'd wear the Reynolds thing.

Delia Or there's the little grey.

Ernest Oh.

Delia Or the blue.

Ernest Ah.

Delia No, that isn't pressed. You decide, darling. Stripy or the other one.

Ernest Er...

Delia Or the grey.

Ernest Er...

Delia Right I've decided, it's the other one. Good. Now, in the spare wardrobe in Trevor's old room on the top shelf, there's a little black handbag. Could you fetch me that?

Delia goes into the bathroom

Ernest Little black handbag, right. (*Looking round*) I don't think you can tell very much from this bedroom. Except the roof's leaking from somewhere.

Ernest goes out

Cross-fade to Nick and Jan's room. Jan comes in in her coat. As soon as Nick, lying in bed, sees her, he groans

Jan Are you all right? (*She kisses him*)

Nick moans

Is it painful?

Nick Amazingly enough, yes.

Jan Are you comfy? (*She picks up a book from the floor and puts it on the bed*)

Nick Not really.

Jan Shall I prop you up a bit? (*She bends him forward roughly, puts a pillow behind him and pushes him back*)

Nick No, no. I'll just—aaaah!

Jan You might want to read.

Nick How can I read? I can't do anything.

Jan Well, your book's there. (*She sits at the dressing-table and brushes her hair*)

Nick Oh, it's maddening. A maddening thing to happen. Why this month. I mean, I'm simply bending down pulling on my socks and bang. It's totally unfair. Why me? I mean, I'm the last person in the world who should be stuck in bed.

Jan Yes...

Nick I'm a naturally active person, aren't I? Aren't I? I have to be on the go. I need to be on the go. I'm going to go mad lying here, you know. I'm going to go off my head, I know it. I've only been here since this morning and I'm dying of boredom. How long did that man say?

Jan Well, a few days. (*She puts on a necklace and earrings*)

Nick We know what that means. I'll be here for Christmas.

Jan Don't be stupid.

Nick That doctor obviously didn't know what he was talking about. Bad luck old chap—a bottle of pills and he's off.

Jan They're supposed to relax you.

Nick All they've done is to give me double vision. Why me? I've got so many things I should be—aaah—should be doing. Did you get hold of the office and tell them about the meeting?

Jan Yes, it's cancelled.

Nick And you sent the telegram to Glasgow?

Jan Yes and I spoke to someone at Shelgrove and told them not to expect you. And I cabled America and asked them to ring this number when convenient. OK?

Nick Right.

Jan (*looking at her watch*) I don't know why you pay a secretary. I won't be long. (*She rises*)

Nick Where are you going?

Jan I told you. Malcolm and Kate's housewarming.

Nick Tonight?

Jan They did invite us both. I phoned and told them what had happened. I said I'd just look in for ten minutes.

Nick What about me?

Jan I won't be long.

Nick You don't want to go to Malcolm and Kate's do you?

Jan I said I would.

Nick What? And sit and look at love's young dream all evening.

Jan There'll be lots of others.

Nick Then they won't miss you, will they?

Jan I said I would.

Nick Well, phone them up.

Jan No, I want to.

Nick Why?

Jan Well.

Nick What on earth for?

Jan Well. If you must know—it's simply that—well. Simply. Susannah is going to be there.

Nick Susannah.

Jan Yes. I wanted to see her. It's a good opportunity and I thought I might . . .

Nick And Trevor.

Jan Yes. Possibly. (*She takes a jacket from the cupboard*)

Nick I should think it's highly probable. Seeing as they're married. Unless he's crippled as well.

Jan Anyway. That's why.

Nick And if it's a choice between Trevor and me, it's going to be Trevor.

Jan No.

Nick Yes.

Jan Not at all.

Nick Yes.

Jan It's just I heard that—well—there's some awful trouble between them. I mean that silly bitch Susannah, she's got no idea at all. She hasn't a clue about Trevor. I know Trevor's impossible sometimes but I think I do know him probably better than anyone . . .

Nick Oh yes, yes.

Jan I think if I talk to them before they do something they'll regret . . .

Nick Like her shooting him.

Jan Don't be silly.

Nick Look, he's a very selfish, very spoilt, self-pitying, self-obsessed . . .

Jan I know, I know.

Nick All right.

Jan Just for ten minutes. I promise. Your book's there. (*She moves to the door*)

Nick Oy!

Jan Mm?

Nick I take it you still prefer me?

Jan I think so. Mostly. (*She kisses him*)

Nick (*wriggling*) Oh.

Jan What is it?

Nick Ah.

Jan What?

Nick This damn bed is full of crumbs.

Jan Crumbs?

Nick From those biscuits. I told you not to give me biscuits.

Jan (*pulling back the side covers and attempting to brush the undersheet beneath him*) OK just a minute, just a minute.

Nick Careful! Careful! CAREFUL!

Jan All right, all right, ALL RIGHT! God, how do they do it? How do these nurses do it? They are saints. I'd go stark raving mad and strangle all the patients. I know I would.

Nick Aaaah! (*He rolls back*)

Jan Nick, will you kindly lie still.

Nick Ah!

Jan There we are. Is that better?

Nick Aah!

Jan And stop that din. It's not that serious.

Nick Hah!

Jan It is not a disc. Nothing is broken. It is just a little tiny muscle.

Nick It is not a little tiny muscle. It is the main motor muscle that runs right up the spinal cord ...

Jan All right. Too bad. Sorry and all that. Won't be long. See you later.

Nick Thanks for the sympathy.

Speaking together

Jan Well, I'm afraid I have the misfortune to be born with only that much sympathy and that's your lot. You've had it all. 'Bye-bye.

Jan exits

Nick Give my love to Trevor ...

Jan (*off*) Oh God.

Nick (*shouting after her, propping himself up on one elbow*) Tell him with me ill in bed, the field's clear for him to ... (*He bumps his head on the bedhead*) Aaah! Oh blimey O'Riley. Why me? Why me?

Cross-fade to Malcolm and Kate's. Malcolm comes in with one of Kate's shoes. He looks for somewhere to hide it. He tucks it down the bottom of the unmade bed. Malcolm sits in the chair innocently. Kate calls off, then enters, holding the other shoe

Kate Malcolm! Malcolm ... I know you're up here, Malcolm. Come on, Malcolm, what have you done with it?

Malcolm What?

Kate My other shoe. What have you done with it?

Malcolm I don't know.

Kate Oh really ... (*Seeing the cardboard package*) What's all this?

Malcolm Ah-ha.

Kate Where did it come from?

Malcolm I got it today.

Kate I didn't see you.

Malcolm You don't see everything.

Kate What is it?

Malcolm A little surprise. Nothing much. A little housewarming present from me to you.

Kate Whatever is it?

Malcolm Later, later. When they've all gone.

Kate Whatever is it? It's an ironing board.

Malcolm An ironing board...

Kate What have you done with my shoe?

Malcolm Shoe? Shoe?

Kate (*giving up*) Oh...

Malcolm (*taking off his shoes*) It's going to be a really good party tonight, I can feel it.

Kate I hope so. Oooh. Something to confess.

Malcolm What?

Kate You know that shelf you put up in the kitchen.

Malcolm Yes.

Kate It's fallen down again.

Malcolm Again...

Kate I was ever so careful.

Malcolm I told you it wasn't designed for great heavy weights.

Kate I only stood the cruet on it. I deliberately didn't go near it in case it fell down. Oh, I'm terribly hot. Have I got time for a bath?

Malcolm Just about.

Kate Now, the food's all going on the big table. Then I've cleared the sideboard for the drinks. And they can put their coats here on the bed—oh look, I haven't made the bed. Where is it then? (*She starts to make the bed*)

Malcolm What?

Kate You know what. My blooming shoe.

Malcolm whistles to himself and starts to take off his sweater

You going to wear your nice shirt?

Malcolm Which one?

Kate Your nice one.

Malcolm All right.

Kate You look nice in that.

Malcolm Yes, it's going to be a really good party. Who've we got coming then?

Kate Oh—everyone—I asked everyone. Except Nick, he can't come.

Malcolm Nick?

Kate Yes, he hurt his back, poor thing.

Malcolm Ah.

Kate Jan phoned me. He hurt it this morning. She's coming though.

Malcolm Good. Good.

Kate And who else is there. Ken and Margaret, of course. And John and Dorothy and Wilfrid and Gareth and Gwen and Mike and Dave and Carole and Dick and Lottie. Gordon and Marge, of course and—er—Susannah and Trevor...

Malcolm Trevor?

Kate Yes.

Malcolm And Susannah?

Kate Yes.

Malcolm Oh dear, oh dear.

Kate Well, I had to. They've had us round twice.

Malcolm I see. Well, that's that isn't it?

Kate Well.

Malcolm That's that. Where is it then?

Kate What?

Malcolm The shirt.

Kate Oh, it's in the airing cupboard. I washed it.

Malcolm Right.

Malcolm goes

Kate Could you turn my bath on?

Malcolm (*off*) Right.

Kate finds her shoe in the bed

Kate Oh really. (*She eyes the present. She sees Malcolm's shoes. She snatches them up and stuffs them into one of the pillowcases*)

Malcolm returns with the shirt

Very funny.

Malcolm Eh?

Kate My shoe. Very funny.

Malcolm Ah.

Kate And I don't want any more foreign bodies in my side of the bed tonight, thank you very much.

Malcolm Foreign bodies?

Kate You know. Hair brushes and all my bottles and jars—you know.

Malcolm Wasn't me.

Kate You and your jokes. Is my bath running?

Malcolm Yes. Now look, you say Jan's coming and Susannah's coming and Trevor's coming?

Kate Yes.

Malcolm (*putting on his shirt*) That's marvellous. If Trevor and Susannah don't have a fight, then it's ten to one Jan and Susannah will have a fight...

Kate I hope not.

Malcolm Well, the first sign of any trouble they're all out, I'm telling you.

This is going to be a good party, I'm not having any of that. (*He has put on his shirt*)

Kate Has that shrunk?

Malcolm I don't know, has it?

Kate It looks as if it's shrunk. Or else you're getting fat.

Kate goes off

Malcolm Fat? You cheeky thing. (*Calling*) Hey, Blodge. Blodge. (*He takes off the shirt*)

Kate (*off*) What?

Malcolm What have you done with my shoes?

Kate (*off*) Ah-ha.

Malcolm What have you done with them? What's she done with them? (*He sees her shoes. He hides them in the bed*)

Kate (*off*) Ooooh!

Malcolm What?

Kate returns, partially undressed

Kate Did you put that brush in my bath?

Malcolm Brush? What brush?

Kate Well, you shouldn't do that. It's very unhygienic. Honestly.

Kate goes. Malcolm, laughing, follows her

Cross-fade to Ernest and Delia's. Delia comes in dressed to go. She looks about her

Delia (*calling*) Ernest! Ernest!

Ernest (*off*) Coming.

Delia Where have you got to?

Ernest enters, dusting himself down

Ernest All ready to go, are you?

Delia Where on earth have you been?

Ernest I was just having a quick squint into the loft. Seeing if I could see any signs. Water's getting in from somewhere.

Delia You're filthy dirty.

Ernest Oh, that's all right. No-one'll notice.

Delia I have. (*She brushes him down*) Now, don't go and overtip tonight, will you.

Ernest Overtip?

Delia You did last year. (*Taking off his jacket and brushing it*) These waiters don't like it.

Ernest I've never heard them object.

Delia I read somewhere it was just as bad form to overtip as it was to undertip. If not worse.

Ernest The bloke last year was pleased enough to take it.

Delia (*putting the jacket on the bed*) The Spanish one. (*She picks up her handbag*)

Ernest Was he Spanish? Smiling all over his face.

Delia You obviously don't know the Spanish. That expression was little short of scornful. Desperately embarrassing. Right, we're off.

Delia goes

Ernest (*following*) I thought he was an Italian, anyway.

Ernest, about to go, stops, returns for his jacket, and exits after Delia

Cross-fade to Nick and Jan's. Nick lying in bed has evidently been reading. He had lain down his book on the eiderdown to rest. He now pulls up the eiderdown round him a little and in doing so, causes his book to fall off the end of the bed

Nick Oh, no, oh no, oh no...

Cross-fade to Malcolm and Kate's. The room is empty. From off a scream from Kate. She rushes in with just a towel round her pursued by Malcolm now shirtless again and brandishing an aerosol can of shaving soap

Kate Now, Malcolm, stop it, do you hear, stop it.

Malcolm You started it.

Kate I did not start it.

Malcolm You splashed me.

Kate All right, I'm sorry.

Malcolm Are you sorry?

Kate Yes, I said I'm sorry.

Malcolm Very sorry?

Kate Yes, very sorry. Now, let me get dressed, Malcolm, please.

Malcolm All right. Splash me again, you're in trouble.

Kate I'm getting dressed in the bathroom, I don't trust you. (*She picks up some clothes and the aerosol can*)

Malcolm Where have you hidden my shoes? (*He looks under the bed*)

Kate sprays his back with the shaving soap, and darts off with a shriek

Malcolm Right, Blodge, you're going to get it Blodge.

Kate (*off*) I've locked the door. You can't come in.

Malcolm I can wait, Blodge, I can wait. I'll get you. I'll get you.

The doorbell rings

Somebody's arrived.

Kate (*off*) What?

Malcolm (*grabbing a petticoat of Kate's from a drawer and wiping off the foam*) Somebody's here. That was the doorbell. (*He slips on his shirt*)

Kate (*off*) Oh no, it wasn't.

Malcolm (*putting on some other shoes*) Want a bet? It was the doorbell.

Kate (*off*) Really? Well, you answer it then.
Malcolm I will.
Kate (*off*) I don't believe you, Malcolm Newton.

Malcolm goes off downstairs

(*Off*) I don't believe you.

Kate comes in still with the towel round her, the soap spray in her hand

Where are you hiding? Malcolm? Malcolm? I can see you, Malcolm. Malcolm, I don't believe you ...

Voices are heard coming upstairs

Oh, my God. (*She runs to the door. She looks round for somewhere. As a last resort, she pulls back the covers and slides into bed*) Ooh! (*She pulls out her shoes from the bed, holds them up then tucks them back under*)

Trevor enters

Malcolm (*off*) Coats just on the bed, Trevor. I'll fix you a drink.
Trevor Right, thanks. (*Seeing Kate*) Ah.
Kate Hallo, Trevor.
Trevor Oh, hallo there. (*He takes off his coat*)
Kate Hallo.
Trevor Are you ill?
Kate No.
Trevor Ah.
Kate I'm just getting changed.
Trevor Ah. Er—Malcolm said it would be all right to put my coat on the bed. Is that OK with you?
Kate Fine.
Trevor (*putting his coat across Kate*) Won't make you too hot, will it?
Kate Uh?
Trevor I mean with all the coats on top of you. Could get a bit hot by the middle of the evening.
Kate Oh no. I'm not staying here. I'm just resting.
Trevor Oh, great.
Kate How are you?
Trevor Fine.
Kate Good. Susannah?
Trevor She's all right. I think.
Kate She downstairs, is she?
Trevor Not that I noticed.
Kate Oh. You didn't come with her then?
Trevor No. We were travelling separately.
Kate Oh. Well...
Trevor Yes. (*He laughs to himself somewhat bitterly*)

Malcolm enters, with two drinks

Malcolm Are you coming down for this drink, Trevor, or are you...(*Seeing Kate*) Oh.

Kate Hallo.

Malcolm What are you doing?

Kate Nothing.

Malcolm Oh. Right. (*Handing Trevor his drink*) Here you are then.

Trevor Thanks.

Malcolm Cheers then.

Trevor Cheers. (*He drinks*)

Malcolm (*to Kate*) You all right?

Kate Fine.

Malcolm Well, what do you think of our place then, Trevor? Our new little love-nest. What's the verdict? Not bad is it? Not bad. Quite nice.

Trevor Yes.

Malcolm Mind you, we've got a lot to do. Masses. This room for one. I mean, it's not properly furnished or anything. Still, we'll get it together. Give us time. Not bad though, is it?

Trevor No.

Malcolm And how are you and—er—well dare I ask—how are you and Susannah these days?

Trevor laughs

Oh, all right. I've said enough. Said enough.

Trevor We're still trying to—work something—out. You know.

Malcolm Good.

Kate Good.

Malcolm Good.

Trevor I don't know how successful we're being but we're trying. You know...

Malcolm Yes—well...

Trevor It's a totally draining experience though. Once you get yourself commited to a—commitment—like Susannah and I have committed ourselves to, you get a situation of a totally outgoing-non-egotistical-giving-ness— a total submerging, you know.

Malcolm Yes, yes.

Kate Yes.

Trevor You feel yourself—being pushed under...

Malcolm Yes.

Trevor As if on top of you were a great—a great ... (*He tails off*)

Kate Yes.

Malcolm Yes.

Kate Yes.

A long pause. Malcolm and Kate wait for Trevor

Trevor (*at length*) Heavy weight. God. (*He turns to face the wall*)

A silence

Kate (*very quietly*) Malcolm, I wonder if you could possibly get my things out of the bathroom.

Malcolm Your what?

Kate My things.

Malcolm Your ... ? Oh, I see. That's what you're up to. Have you got nothing on under there?

Kate (*embarrassed*) No.

Malcolm (*laughing*) Do you hear that, Trevor?

Trevor (*turning*) Eh?

Malcolm She's got nothing on under there.

Trevor No, no.

Malcolm Hey hey! Wait there, I'll ...

The doorbell rings

Ah, somebody else. Hang on.

Malcolm darts out

Kate (*calling after him vainly*) Could you fetch my clothes before you ... Trevor, I'm going to have to ask you in a minute if you'd mind ... Trevor.

Trevor Sorry, Kath. I was miles away. I'm sorry. Kath, listen.

Kate Kate, yes.

Trevor I was just thinking, what is the point of it all really. You and I. Take you and me. We start out in this world with the innocence of children. We start our lives like little children.

Kate Well, we are.

Trevor Have you ever studied children at close range?

Kate Oh yes. I like children.

Trevor I have. You have a close look at them sometime.

Kate I have.

Trevor Really closely. And then look at yourself. You'll be appalled at what's happened to you, Kath. And this—this is the test. You try and think of three—I'm only asking for three—three good reasons why you shouldn't throw yourself out of that window here and now.

Kate I haven't got any clothes on.

Trevor Three good reasons, eh.

Kate Yes.

Trevor See what I mean?

Kate Yes, I follow your reasoning.

Trevor You do?

Kate Yes. I don't agree with it but I think I can follow it.

Trevor You either don't think things out at all or you're lucky, Kath. I'll give you the benefit of the doubt.

Malcolm enters with a pile of coats. He also has Kate's clothes

Malcolm Whole load of people. Mike, Dave, Graham and Anna, Gareth and Gwen, Bob and Terry ... Oh, Trevor.

Trevor Mm?

Malcolm Now listen, Susannah's arrived.

Trevor Oh.

Malcolm Now, there's a house rule tonight. No arguments with your own wife. Anybody else's wife but not your own, all right?

Trevor I should tell her—not me.

Malcolm Now, Trevor, one word you're out.

Trevor I'll try, Malcolm I'll try.

Trevor goes

Malcolm I must say Susannah seems in good form. I opened the door to her, she burst into tears and ran straight into the bathroom. Oh well, press on ... Hurry up and come down. They're all arriving.

Kate I will. Are those my clothes?

Malcolm Oh yes—here. (*He throws them to her*)

Kate At last. (*She snatches them gratefully*)

Malcolm goes out to the hall

Malcolm (*calling*) John ... Brian ... Dave. Don't hang them there. It wasn't designed to take any sort of weight. Bring them up here. Put them on the bed.

Kate Oh ... (*She dives under the bedclothes and starts to dress*)

Cross-fade to Nick

Nick (*in extreme frustration*) Aaah—aaah—aaaaah! (*He gets up on his elbows to see if he can see his book. In pain*) Ah! (*Nick rolls over on to his front. He slithers sideways out of bed and finally lands on the floor on all fours with a clump. He yells again. He begins laboriously to crawl round to the end of the bed to reach his book*) Ah-ha. Gotcha. (*He tries to get back on to the bed. He can't make it. He brings the eiderdown slithering down on top of him*) Oh no. Jan. Help. *Help.* (*He lies on the floor helplessly*) Why me? Why me?

Cross-fade to Malcolm and Kate's. Malcolm enters with more coats which he throws on the bed. Kate is hidden beneath them

Malcolm (*calling behind him*) Just along the passage there, Joan. It's the blue door. (*He turns to go*)

Susannah comes in, passing Malcolm

Just leave your coat on the bed, would you, Susannah? Just on the bed there.

Susannah I didn't realize there were going to be so many people.

Malcolm It's a party, my darling, what do you expect.

Susannah Yes. (*She puts her coat on the bed*)

Malcolm goes

(*Taking a deep breath*) I am confident in myself. I have confidence in myself. I am not unattractive. I am attractive. People still find me attractive. I am not afraid of people. People are not frightening. There is nothing to be frightened of.

During this, Kate's head slowly emerges from under the sheets. She gapes at Susannah in wonderment. Susannah sees her, and jumps very nervously

Kate Hallo. Sorry. I didn't mean to startle you.

Susannah I was just doing my—exercises. I do them whenever I'm alone. Or when I feel alone. They help.

Kate Oh yes.

Susannah Trevor's here, I suppose?

Kate Yes, yes. (*She gets out of bed*)

Susannah He hasn't said hallo to me, I notice. No doubt he's better things to occupy him.

Kate Well . . .

Susannah I see that woman's here.

Kate Who's that? (*She picks up her shoes*)

Susannah Whatever her name is. Jan.

Kate Oh, Jan. Yes. Poor old Nick's in bed. He's ill.

Susannah Oh. Is he? How lucky for her.

Kate (*moving to the door*) Excuse me. I must pop down. See things are all right.

Susannah Kate.

Kate Yes?

Susannah Just a moment.

Kate Yes?

Susannah Tell me something. Do you and Malcolm still have—how are you and Malcolm?

Kate Oh, very well.

Susannah Truly?

Kate Yes.

Susannah You can be honest, you know.

Kate Yes. Well. We have a bit of a laugh. You know.

The doorbell rings

Oh, there's the . . .

Susannah I don't know if you know it but things for Trevor and I have gone totally wrong.

Kate Yes, I heard a rumour.

Susannah I'm sure everyone's heard a rumour. We're neither of us very good at—conventional cover-ups. Is it still exciting for you?

Kate What?

Susannah God, Trevor used to excite me. I was so excited by that man. Do you know what it feels like to be really excited?

Kate Yes, yes, I think so.

Susannah When we weren't actually physically here in the bed—you know, making love—I felt empty—utterly incomplete.

Kate Yes, it is nice sometimes, isn't it . . .

Susannah And now. Now, it's a desert. We hardly touch, you know.

Kate Oh.

Susannah I think I actually revolt him.

Kate Oh, surely not.

Susannah I sometimes feel that. Suddenly I've lost all my identity. Some mornings, who am I, I say. Who am I? And I don't know. I terrify myself. (*Leaning towards Kate confidentially*) I saw this girl in the street the other day—about my age—a little bit younger. Do you know, I felt aroused by her. Attracted.

Kate Oh.

Susannah Isn't that terrifying?

Kate (*gently backing away*) Yes.

Susannah Not that the feeling in itself is terrifying. I don't believe the feeling in itself is wrong but what it means is that all the things I used to think I knew about myself I no longer know.

Kate Yes, yes.

Susannah I suppose you're beautifully uncomplicated, Kate.

Kate Yes, I think so. Look, I must pop down. Do you want to . . .?

Susannah Could I just lie down for a moment?

Kate Oh yes, yes, do. Move the coats.

Susannah Thanks. I'll pluck up courage in a minute. I'm sorry, I'm being absolutely useless.

Kate No, no, no. Not at all. (*Half-way out of the door*) See you in a minute.

Susannah Yes.

Kate goes

Susannah clears a few coats from one side of the bed. Dramatically, she throws herself back on to the pillow. She strikes her head. She discovers the boots in the pillowcase. She looks puzzled. She lies back again

Cross-fade to Nick

Nick (*in the same position as before*) Help . . .

Cross-fade to Delia and Ernest. Delia and Ernest return from their meal

Ernest Well, that place has certainly gone off.

Delia You can say that again. Disastrous meal.

Ernest Three times as expensive too.

Delia Yes. I noticed you deliberately undertipped.

Ernest (*taking off his watch*) I didn't deliberately undertip. I just didn't bring enough money with me. (*He puts his keys and change on the bedside table*)

Delia That Spaniard looked even more miserable than last year.

Ernest Serve him right. Highway robbery.

Delia And that asparagus was out of a tin.

Ernest That wasn't bad.

Delia No, it was quite nice but it was out of a tin.

Ernest Oh yes, certainly out of a tin.

Delia I've never felt so over-dressed in my life. All those young men, none of them with a tie. And all those girls in slacks.

Ernest Well, they didn't bother me. (*He starts to take off his shoes*)

Delia It's all those labels sewn all over their bottoms and places I find so off-putting. I mean, nobody can seriously want to read people's bottoms. I mean, one girl had reams.

Ernest I think that's the thing, isn't it?

Delia When I was their age, I spent all my time making sure nobody could read my labels. I mean, we would rather have died than show a label.

Ernest We used to show the odd label, I think. On the inside of the jacket. Let the other chap see you had a tailor. Ah well, back to worrying about the roof, I suppose.

Delia (*drawing the window curtains*) I don't know about you but I'm still feeling distinctly peckish.

Ernest Are you? Yes, I am a bit. (*He loosens his tie*)

Delia There's some sardines downstairs.

Ernest Sardines. That sounds attractive.

Delia On toast?

Ernest Rather. Let's go the whole hog if we're going to.

Delia Tell you what...

Ernest Um?

Delia Let's be really really wicked...

Ernest Eh?

Delia Let's eat them in bed.

Ernest In bed?

Delia Sardines on toast in bed, do you remember?

Ernest Good Lord, yes. You've got a memory. Sardines on toast in bed, yes.

Delia I was expecting Trevor...

Ernest That's right. Are you sure it wasn't baked beans?

Delia No, not baked beans. Sardines.

Ernest Yes, quite right. Sardines. All right, we'll go one better. I'll go and hot them up while you get into your jim-jams.

Delia Oh, all right. (*She picks up her handbag*)

Ernest No sooner said...

Delia What fun.

Ernest Off you go

Delia goes into the bathroom. Ernest takes his pyjamas from under his pillow and goes off the other way

Cross-fade to Malcolm and Kate's. Susannah is still on the bed. Kate ushers in Trevor

Kate She's in here, Trevor, having a lie down. Here he is, Susannah. Found him for you.

Kate exits, shutting the door

Trevor Tired?

Susannah No.

Trevor If you're tired, you shouldn't have come.

Susannah If I listened to you I wouldn't go anywhere at all. Mind you, you'd prefer that I'm sure. (*Pause*) You don't have to stay up here with me, you know. I'm very used to being on my own. I'm sure there's lots of people down there you'd rather be talking to.

Trevor I came up to see if you were all right.

Susannah You came up because Kate told you to come up. You'd never have come near me all evening if you could possibly have avoided it.

Trevor Look, don't get worked up. What are you getting worked up about?

Susannah Because I've every reason to be worked up.

Trevor Quieten down.

Pause

Susannah You're a fine one to talk.

Trevor What?

Susannah If people had seen you earlier this evening...

Trevor Well...

Sussanah Driving here and leaving me to walk.

Trevor I didn't think you were coming.

Susannah You knew I was coming.

Trevor I thought you wanted to stay behind.

Susannah You knew perfectly well I was coming.

Trevor Then why did you lock yourself in the bedroom?

Susannah Because I didn't want you in there.

Trevor What? In case I saw you changing? Good gracious. Husband sees his wife changing. I don't know what it is you're hiding but I bet it's fantastic.

Susannah You really are coarse, aren't you? Coarse and violent.

Trevor You're the one who makes me violent. I was a pacifist before I met you.

Susannah I wish I'd listened to that man.

Trevor What man?

Susannah That man we consulteu just before we were married. The one who did the palm readings.

Trevor What, him?

Susannah He told me you were potentially a violent person. He was absolutely right. You've broken all my things. All my things I brought from home. All my china animals.

Trevor I told you, I'm sorry, I'll buy you some more.

Susannah I don't want some more. I wanted those.

Trevor I didn't mean to break them.

Susannah Then why did you throw a chair at them if you didn't mean to break them?

Trevor I don't know. I just felt like throwing a chair, that's all. No law against throwing chairs is there? It was my chair.

Susannah Potentially violent. That's what he said. That man.

Trevor He was an idiot.

Susannah No, he wasn't. My mother always went to him.

Trevor (*moving to the bed*) He told me I had a natural mechanical aptitude. I can't even put the plug on the Hoover. (*Lying on the bed*) Well anyway, the one good thing about this party...

Susannah What?

Trevor At least we're both lying on the same bed.

Susannah (*lunging at him with a fist*) You rotten...

Trevor Ah, now who's violent?

Susannah (*hailing blows upon him*) You destroy everything, don't you? Everything. Everything.

Trevor (*laughing as he covers up from her blows*) What are you doing now?

Susannah (*furiously*) Oh, I could so easily—oh—oh—oh.

Trevor Ow! Now, stop it. Stop it.

Eventually he pushes her off and she slips on to the floor

Susannah Ow. You great bully.

Trevor Now, stop it. Before you're sorry.

Susannah (*getting up*) I'm not sorry. I am not sorry. (*She snatches up the table lamp*)

Trevor Now, put that down. Put it down. It's not yours.

Susannah Get away, get away, get away.

Trevor approaches her. She lunges at him with the lamp. He grabs her wrist. He loses his balance. They both land on the bed, locked in mortal combat. Fighting for serious now, they roll on to the floor clawing and tugging at hair

Malcolm enters with a plate of Cornish pasties

Malcolm Right. Who's for Cornish pasties ... (*Seeing them*) Oh no. Now, break it up. Break it up. That table lamp won't take that sort of treatment. (*Putting the Cornish pasties on the floor*) Now, come on. Trevor! Susannah! Come on, break it up. (*He attempts to pull them apart*)

Kate appears in the doorway

Kate (*speaking above the din*) The plaster's coming down. What's happening?

Malcolm Come on, give us a hand. Give us a hand here. You pull her. I'll pull him. Pull, woman, pull.

Kate I am pulling.

Trevor and Susannah are separated. They stand panting, staring at each other; Kate holding Susannah, Malcolm holding Trevor

Malcolm Now, calm down. Do you hear? Calm down, both of you. Calm down. That's it.

Kate releases Susannah

Now, both of you, take a deep breath.

With renewed energy, Susannah suddenly clouts Trevor with the table lamp

Kate	Stop it, stop it, Susannah...		*Speaking*
Malcolm	Stop that at once.		*together*
Trevor	Ow.		

Susannah rushes out

Trevor Right—all right. (*Wrenching free from Malcolm*) Right.

Trevor chases out after Susannah

There are sounds of crashes downstairs

Kate Malcolm, do something, please.

Malcolm Right. I am now personally going to drop him straight off our roof on to his head.

Malcolm goes out

Kate (*anxiously following him to the doorway and watching*) Oh now, Malcolm, don't you start. You must be the one to keep calm, Malcolm. Don't you start. (*Picking up the Cornish pasties*) Malcolm—Malcolm ... (*She hops up and down in agitation*)

Malcolm returns half-carrying Trevor

Malcolm (*hurling him into the room*) Right, you get your coat. Do you hear? Get your coat. Then you're out. Straight out, mate. Come along, Kate.

Malcolm goes out

Kate Right. (*Slipping a Cornish pasty on to the corner of the bed*) I'll leave you one of these.

Kate goes out

Trevor sits on the bed recovering his breath. He feels his head

Trevor Oooh.

Jan comes in. She glances at him briefly. She looks for her coat, picking the others off the floor

Jan I hope you're thoroughly ashamed of yourself. Both of you. (*Pause*) God, to think I nearly married you. What an escape.

Trevor (*muttering*) She started that one. She started that one.

Jan I hoped that after I left you, you might have learnt to grow up. It appears that you're more retarded than ever. I mean, I realized that as long as I was there to look after you, make all your decisions you could never make, you hadn't a chance ...

Trevor God, my head.
Jan When are you going to grow up, Trevor?

Malcolm enters

Malcolm Excuse me, please. (*Snatching up coats*) Gordon's coat. Marge's coat. Mike and Dave's coats. Gwen's coat. (*To Trevor*) I told you, out.

Malcolm goes

Jan Well?
Trevor (*putting his half-eaten pastie on the box*) Just because I have an unfortunate marriage, I'm not necessarily an idiot. I try. I try all the time.
Jan Like you did with me.
Trevor I particularly tried with you. I was always working flat out to make a go of it.
Jan I don't think you noticed half the time if I was there or not.
Trevor I did.
Jan Which is why I left. That didn't seem to bother you either.
Trevor What do you mean? I was annihilated. What are you talking about? I needed you.
Jan Yes. I realized that from the way you came running after me.
Trevor I thought you'd be back.
Jan No, thank you.
Trevor Never mind, eh. You're all right.
Jan Perfectly.
Trevor Safe and secure with Nick.
Jan That's right.
Trevor Some of us aren't so lucky.

Malcolm enters

Malcolm Excuse me. John's coat. Ken's coat. Margaret's coat. Dorothy's coat. (*To Trevor*) This is your last warning.

Malcolm goes

Jan You see? You can't go anywhere.
Trevor I'm a destroyer.
Jan True.
Trevor Susannah said that. I destroy everything. She's right. I even destroyed you.
Jan No, you didn't.
Trevor Destroyed you. So you go out and in desperation, you marry the first man you happen to meet.
Jan That's not very fair to Nick.
Trevor No, well...
Jan I happen to love Nick.

Trevor Like you loved me.

Jan No, not like I loved you. Like I love Nick. Quite different. Thank goodness. I can just about cope with Nick. I don't think I could ever have coped with you.

Malcolm enters

Malcolm Bob's coat. Terry's coat. Anna's coat. Graham's coat. (*Turning to Trevor, livid*) You've ruined this party. You realize that, don't you?

Trevor Have I?

Malcolm You and that wife of yours. You've ruined fifty people's evening down there.

Trevor Well, I'm sorry

Malcolm What's the point in being sorry now, mate.

Jan Malcolm, don't.

Malcolm Him and his batty bloody wife. Sitting there in the middle of the front room crying her eyes out she is. If I had my way I'd have you both locked up for good ... They've all gone home, every one of them...

Jan Malcolm.

Malcolm I'm sorry, Jan. Every one of them. I hope you're satisfied.

Malcolm slams out

Trevor I might have improved if you'd stayed with me. I mean, with you, Jan, I ... You see, Susannah I can't get near. She's incapable of giving. She won't give.

Jan Perhaps you don't deserve anything.

Trevor Oh, what does that mean?

Jan It means that before anyone's prepared to give anything, they want to make sure first that the person they're giving it to is not going to hurl it back at their heads the first time he chooses to lose his temper. You'll have to learn to treat people properly. There you are. End of lecture. Now I'm going home.

Trevor I treated you properly.

Jan No, you didn't.

Trevor Not ever?

Jan No.

Trevor Never at all?

Jan Not really.

Trevor No?

Jan No.

Trevor kisses Jan. She responds

Kate enters

Kate Oh. It's all right, Susannah, I'll bring it down. I'll bring it down to you.

Susannah enters

Susannah That's all right. (*A swift glance at Trevor and Jan, she picks up her coat and puts it on*)
Trevor Er ...
Jan Susannah ...

Susannah goes out

Jan Oh God.
Kate Oh dear.

Trevor sinks on to the floor, his head in his hands

Jan Look, can you go after her, Trevor, quickly ... No, silly question. Oh well, I've really done it now. Sorry, Kate. I'll have to leave you with it. I'd better get back to Nick.
Kate Right.
Jan Good night all.

Jan goes

Kate 'Night. Malcolm's down there seeing them off.
Jan (*off*) OK.
Kate Oh dear. (*She looks at Trevor*) Oh dear. (*She shuts the door*) Oh dear, oh dear. Susannah's driving. I hope she gets home all right.
Trevor I don't know where I'm going to go.
Kate How do you mean?
Trevor I can't go home.
Kate Can't you?
Trevor How can I go home ...?

A pause

Kate We've got the little bedroom in the back. It isn't furnished or anything but we've got a camp bed.
Trevor (*clutching at Kate's dress*) You're a true friend, Kath.
Kate Kate, yes.
Trevor (*letting go of the dress*) Sorry about your party.
Kate Oh well—get to bed early, won't we? I'll go and make the bed up for you. (*She points at the box*) Look at this. Malcolm's surprise for me. In there. Malcolm's surprise.
Trevor Oh.
Kate I don't know what it is.

Malcolm enters

Malcolm Right, that's it. End of party. All gone. (*Seeing Trevor*) Oh. You're still here, are you? Now I warned you ...
Kate Malcolm ...
Malcolm (*picking up Trevor's coat*) This your coat?
Kate Malcolm ...

Malcolm Eh?
Kate I've said he could stay.
Malcolm Stay?
Kate Just for the night.
Malcolm Who? Trevor? You're joking. Home.
Kate He's got nowhere to go, Malcolm. He'll have to stay.
Malcolm He's got a home hasn't he? Let him go to it.
Kate He can't.
Malcolm All I know is he's not staying here...

Trevor picks up the pastie and starts to eat it

Kate I'm sorry, Malcolm, he'll have to stay.
Malcolm Not under my roof. Not after his behaviour tonight.
Kate I'm sorry but he is.
Malcolm I'm sorry but he isn't.
Kate Look, there's no point in arguing.
Malcolm No. Quite. Out...
Kate No, I'm sorry.
Malcolm Yes, I'm sorry too. I'm very sorry. He is not staying in this house
and that is final.
Kate Oh yes he is, and that is also final.

Pause

Malcolm (*throwing Trevor's coat on the floor*) All right, all right.
Kate Where are you going?
Malcolm I'll tell you this much. If he is staying then I am definitely not staying.
Kate Now, Malcolm.
Malcolm And that, my love, is that. I am not staying if he is staying so take
your choice.

Malcolm goes, slamming the door

Kate Oh.

A door slams

Kate Oh.
Trevor Sorry.
Kate Oh.
Trevor Where's he gone?
Kate (*snapping*) I don't know where he's gone, you damn fool.
Trevor Oh. Well.
Kate He'll be back. I'll make up your bed.
Trevor Thanks. Er—Kath ...
Kate (*shouting*) Kate. My name is Kate.
Trevor Oh. Yes. Sorry.
Kate Now. Sheets.
Trevor Look. I must get things cleared up before I go to bed.
Kate How do you mean?

Trevor Well, with Jan and Nick, you see.
Kate Jan and Nick?
Trevor Well, it was my fault and—word's bound to get back to Nick—and—
he'll feel badly—and he might take it out on Jan—I wouldn't want that.
Kate Who's going to tell Nick?
Trevor Well, Susannah for one.
Kate Oh. Might she?
Trevor She might.
Kate Oh. Are you going round tonight?
Trevor I'd better.
Kate You could phone.
Trevor Oh no. Face to face stuff this. Has to be.
Kate Don't forget your coat. (*She helps him into it*)
Trevor Don't wait up. I'll let myself in.
Kate Oh yes, you'd better have a key—oh no, we haven't had another one
cut yet. There's only Malcolm's.
Trevor Oh. Well, I won't be long.
Kate It's all right, I'll wait up.
Trevor You're really great, Kate. Thanks.
Kate That's all right. That coat's very big on you, isn't it?
Trevor I don't think it's mine.
Kate Oh. Well, it's the only one left. You'd better take that one.
Trevor Yes. Right. See you later.

Trevor goes

Kate 'Bye. (*She sits on the bed looking worried*)

*Trevor returns in silence, puts the remains of the pastie on the cabinet, and
goes*

*Cross-fade to Ernest and Delia's. Delia, in her dressing-gown, sits in front of
her mirror and starts to remove her make-up. Ernest enters with two plates of
pilchards on toast*

Ernest Grub up.
Delia Just a minute.
Ernest It'll get cold.
Delia I've just got to take this off.
Ernest You can do that afterwards.
Delia I'm not getting into bed with my make-up on, darling. It may look
beautiful in the films but they don't have to worry about laundry bills.
Ernest Oh well. Spot of bad news, anyway.
Delia Bad news?
Ernest Sardines were not in evidence. I had to settle for pilchards.
Delia Pilchards? Oh...
Ernest Don't you like pilchards?
Delia Well, not as much.
Ernest (*putting one plate on a bedside table*) Similar. Both fish, anyway.

Delia Yes.

Ernest You had them in stock. I assumed you liked them.

Delia I don't necessarily like everything I buy. Those were just stores. For an emergency.

Ernest (*putting the other plate on the other table*) Ah, the old siege stores, eh?

Delia I bought a little of everything. I think there's even some tinned red cabbage and I certainly don't intend to eat that.

Ernest (*taking off his dressing-gown*) Oh well, I'll wolf the lot then shall I?

Delia No, no, leave me a little.

Ernest Right. (*He slides into bed*) Aaah Didn't put the blanket on, did we?

Delia Nor we did.

Ernest Ah. Woof. Down you go. (*He shoves his feet into the bed*) Ah, this is nice. What better way to end a day? Listening to the rain gushing through our roof ... (*He starts to eat*)

Delia It's not raining surely?

Ernest Metaphorical. These aren't bad at all. You know, I think I could become a pilchard man in time.

Delia I'll phone Susannah tomorrow to see how they're getting on.

Ernest Good idea. I think we're in imminent need of a hot water bottle here, you know.

Delia Oh yes.

Ernest Bearing in mind the normal running temperature of your feet.

Delia Not my fault. Most women have cold feet. It's circulation.

Ernest I wouldn't know about that. I haven't sampled that many.

Delia The girls at school did. Well, not the younger ones. Younger girls have very hot feet. Like little boys. But when we got to the sixth form, we all found we had cold feet. I think it's something to do with—maturing.

Ernest Very curious. Chaps I shared a hut with in the army all had overwhelmingly hot feet...

Delia I can imagine. (*She takes off her dressing gown*)

Ernest Yes, I pronounce these pilchards a success.

Delia Jolly good. Right, here I come. (*She gets into bed*)

Ernest Stand by for cold feet.

Delia Darling, you're getting fish on the sheet. (*She gives him some tissues from the bedside table*)

Ernest Oh, sorry.

Delia Now we're going to reek of fish all night. I don't think this was a terribly bright idea of someone's.

Ernest Oh well. You only live once. What the hell.

Delia Well, it's on your side. You have to put up with it. (*She eats*) Oh yes, they're quite pleasant aren't they? Not up to sardines, but not bad.

Ernest They got my vote.

Delia At least we're in for a reasonably early night.

Ernest Yes.

Delia Sunday tomorrow, we can lie in.

Ernest Go for a walk later on if you like.

Delia That'd be nice.

Ernest If unwet.

Delia Rather.
Ernest Otherwise we'll both be crouching in the rafters with buckets.
Delia God forbid.

Cross-fade to Nick and Jan's. Nick is still lying on the floor. Jan arrives back

Jan Nick. Nick . . .
Nick Aaaah.
Jan (*seeing him*) Darling, what are you doing?
Nick What do you think I'm doing? I've been lying here for hours.
Jan Oh, darling. How did you get there?
Nick I dropped my book.
Jan (*trying to find a way to get him up*) Well, let me—how do I get you —
    shall I . . .?
Nick No, no. Don't do that. Let me climb up you.
Jan Right.
Nick Can you take the weight?
Jan Hang on. Right. (*She takes his arms and pulls*)
Nick Hup—right—hold steady. Steady . . .
Jan I'm trying. I'm trying.
Nick Keep still.
Jan You are very heavy.
Nick Right. Nearly there.
Jan Oh . . .
Nick What?
Jan You're on my foot.
Nick All right.
Jan Please get off my foot.
Nick I will. Wait a minute.
Jan Oh dear God, my foot.
Nick Right. Hold on, hold on.

*Jan loses her balance. They both crash on to the bed. Nick falling across Jan
who is trapped underneath him*

    Aaaaah. Aaaah. Aaaah.
Jan Aaaaah.
Nick Aaaah.
Jan Oh, that was agony.
Nick Aaaaah.
Jan Can you get off me, darling?
Nick I cannot move at all. Ever again.
Jan Well, try to move. I'm trapped.
Nick I'm sorry. If I could move I would but I'm physically incapable of mov-
    ing.
Jan Can you get off my ribs? You're so heavy.
Nick I am not heavy. I am the correct weight for a man of my height.
Jan Well, that is still bloody heavy. (*Easing herself slowly underneath him*)
    Hang on, I'll try and—oouf. (*She rests*)
Nick Did you have a nice evening?

Jan No.

Nick Didn't think you would. Serve you right for going.

Jan Thank you. Here we go again. (*She renews her efforts to slide from under him*) Huh. Huh.—hoo—hup—oh dear God. This is going to take all night. Can't you even roll over?

Nick Ha ha...

Jan Well, can you be a gentleman and take your weight on your elbows?

Nick No. That puts a direct strain on all the muscles all the way ...

Jan All right. Sorry. Oh dear. (*She laughs*) We're going to be like this for ever. People will find us in years to come. They'll all jump to the wrong conclusions, failing to realize what a rare occurrence this is. Us together on the bed.

Nick There's no need to get unpleasant.

Jan Sorry.

Nick I've been working very hard lately.

Jan Yes, all right, I'm sorry.

Nick And now thanks to my back, we may have to get someone in for you. Try again.

Jan Humphh—oh—I'm so weak.

Nick You're telling me.

Jan Nick.

Nick Mmm?

Jan While I've got your attention...

Nick Mm?

Jan I want to tell you something.

Nick I can hardly avoid listening.

Jan Good. I'm telling you because a I want to tell you and b I've a feeling if I don't a certain person will be phoning you up very shortly to tell you herself.

Nick Who?

Jan Susannah.

Nick Susannah?

Jan Well, very simply—or not very simply—I had a long talk to Trevor.

Nick Ah-ha...

Jan Which culminated in Trevor kissing me.

Nick I see.

Jan And to be perfectly honest, with me kissing Trevor.

Nick Just kissing him?

Jan Yes. Nothing else.

Nick Oh, well. Hope you enjoyed it.

Jan Yes I did, thank you.

Nick Good. I hope you don't want me to start jumping about with rage.

Jan No. Not at all. Not at all. (*She slides out from under him*) Right. Now let's get you into bed. (*Without a lot of ceremony*) Come on. (*She pushes him up the bed by his knees*)

Nick Careful, careful.

Jan Come on, it doesn't hurt.

Nick Don't start taking it out on me just because...

Jan I'm not taking it out on anyone.
Nick As you say, you only kissed him. If you want me to knock you about, you'll have to wait until I'm better.
Jan I don't want anything, thank you.
Nick You only kissed him.
Jan Yes, quite. I went to bed with all the other men at the party but I only kissed Trevor.
Nick Oh well, that's all right. I had three or four women in while you were out actually. That explains the back.
Jan (*unamused*) There you are.
Nick Thank you. Can I have my book, please?

Jan puts the book on Nick's stomach, then slams her hand down on the book

Jan There you are.
Nick Thank you.
Jan Happy?
Nick Thank you.
Jan (*pounding the bed rail in fury and frustration*) Aaarrrggh!
Nick Did you say something?
Jan I'm going to wash my hair. (*She picks up a hair-dryer from the dressing table*)
Nick Wash your hair?
Jan Yes.
Nick It's half past twelve.
Jan So what.

Jan goes

Nick (*mildly amused as she goes out*) Dear, dear, dear ...

Cross-fade to Malcolm and Kate's. Kate wanders in. She sits unhappily. Malcolm returns

Malcolm Hallo.
Kate Oh, Malcolm.
Malcolm Got a bit churned up. (*He shuts the door*)
Kate Yes, I know. I understand. (*Pause*) They left mountains of food.
Malcolm (*sitting on the bed*) Never mind. (*Pause*) I was sitting in the car, that's all.
Kate I'm glad you've come in. (*She sits next to him*)
Malcolm Oh yes. Well. As soon as I saw you'd turfed Trevor out, I came back.
Kate Oh. Well...
Malcolm What? (*He lies back*)
Kate He's coming back.
Malcolm (*sitting up*) Coming back? Here?
Kate Yes, he's just gone round to see Jan and Nick.
Malcolm Jan and Nick?
Kate Yes.

Malcolm Hasn't he done enough damage?
Kate Well, he wanted to sort things out.
Malcolm And you told him he could come back here?
Kate Yes.
Malcolm Well, how's he going to get in?
Kate I said I'd wait up.
Malcolm You are soft in the head, you know that don't you?
Kate Probably.
Malcolm (*rising*) We're not going to get much sleep round here tonight then. Are we?
Kate I don't know.
Malcolm (*rolling up his sleeves*) In that case ...
Kate What are you doing?
Malcolm (*hauling out the cardboard box*) I'll make a start on this. If you don't come to bed, I can't sleep so I might as well do *something* useful.
Kate What is that?
Malcolm Surprise. You'll see. I'll just fetch the tool kit. (*He goes to the door*) Only take me fifteen minutes. I'll put it together for you.
Kate Oh lovely ...

Malcolm goes, closing the door

Cross-fade to Ernest and Delia's

Delia I feel as if I'm sleeping on board a herring trawler. This whole room reeks of fish.
Ernest We'll get used to it.
Delia I doubt it.
Ernest Want the light out?
Delia In a minute.
Ernest Shall I read to you for a bit?
Delia If you like. I'll go to sleep as soon as you start. You have been warned.
Ernest Oh well. (*He puts on his spectacles*)
Delia You have a very soporific reading manner.
Ernest Probably. I'll read you a bit of this, shall I?
Delia What is it?
Ernest *Tom Brown's Schooldays.*
Delia I thought you'd read that.
Ernest Oh yes, rather. Always worth a re-read. Marvellous stuff. Now then. "Tom was detained in school a few minutes after the rest, and on coming out into the quadrangle, the first thing he saw was a small ring of boys, applauding Williams, who was holding Arthur by the collar. 'There, you young sneak,' said he, giving Arthur a cuff on the head with his other hand; 'what made you say that—' 'Hallo!' said Tom, shouldering into the crowd ..."
Delia I can't follow a word of this.
Ernest Perfectly clear.
Delia Not to me. Who are all these people?

Ernest Well, we do have the disadvantage of starting on page two hundred and fifty-six. But I'm damned if I'm going all the way back to the beginning just so you can go to sleep. Shall I carry on?

Delia If you want to.

Ernest I'm asking you. I don't mind.

Delia Oh yes, carry on for goodness sake. (*She gets under the covers*) Only not too loud.

Ernest "'Hallo!' said Tom, shouldering into the crowd; 'you drop that, Williams; you shan't touch him.' 'Who'll stop me?' said the Slogger, raising his hand again . . .'"

The doorbell rings

Good heavens.

Delia (*sitting up*) Was that the doorbell?

Ernest Sounded like it.

Delia (*looking at her clock*) It's twenty to one. Have a look and see who it is.

Ernest Yes, all right. (*He gets out of bed and puts on his dressing-gown and slippers*)

Delia Look out of the window.

Ernest Right. (*He goes to the window*)

The lights come up also on Nick and Jan's. As Jan comes back into the room, her hair in a towel, the doorbell rings

Jan What was that?

Nick Front door.

Jan Funny.

Nick Have a look.

Jan (*going to the window*) Right.

Ernest Looks suspiciously like Susannah.

Delia Oh Lord . . .

Jan (*in a low voice*) I think it's Trevor.

Nick Oh no. Why me? Why me?

As Ernest and Jan go towards their respective front doors the Lights come up on Malcolm and Kate's, with a sight of Malcolm starting to unpack his assemble-it-yourself bedroom surprise: a great clattering and clanking of tools. Kate sits on the bed watching

Malcolm Ah! Ha!

CURTAIN

ACT II

The same. A few moments later

The Lights are up on all three rooms

Malcolm and Kate's room is now strewn with tools from his tool-box and littered with wrapping-paper removed from the easy-to-assemble-it-yourself dressing-table which is scattered about in various pieces. Malcolm has unfurled a plan and is crouching on the floor studying it. Kate sits on the bed watching

Nick is in bed as usual

Delia is in bed

Kate It's going to be lovely when it's all put together.
Malcolm As soon as I've made head or tail of this plan. (*He studies it*)

Ernest returns to Delia

Ernest She's—er—just gone in the bathroom downstairs.
Delia I suppose I'll have to get up. (*She does so, and puts on her slippers and dressing-gown*)
Ernest Yes, well, there's no need to go downstairs—it's a bit parky. I told her to come up here when she's ready. Then you can talk.
Delia Does she want to talk to me?
Ernest Presumably. I can't think of anyone else she'd want to talk to.
Delia No.
Ernest She seems in a rather—distraught state. Could be a long session. Shall I make us some cocoa?
Delia Yes. I'd better try and make myself reasonably presentable.

Delia goes to the bathroom. Ernest goes back downstairs

The Lights fade on Ernest and Delia's

Trevor enters with Jan, still with a towel round her head

Jan It's Trevor, darling.
Nick (*without much geniality*) Good Lord.
Trevor Hi, Nick.
Jan Nice coat. Is it new?
Trevor Er—yes.
Jan Smart.

Nick Is there just the one of you in it, or are there more?
Trevor What?
Jan Let me take it.
Trevor Thanks. (*He takes off his coat*)
Nick What can we do for you?
Jan Sit down. Trevor. (*She takes the coat*)
Trevor Thanks.
Nick At ten to one in the morning.
Trevor Well—(*he looks at Jan*)—well . . .
Jan Would you rather I wasn't here?
Trevor Well . . .
Jan It's all right, I'll make some tea. Then I've got to dry my hair.
Trevor Right. Thanks.

Jan goes

Trevor sits brooding. Nick waits

Malcolm I'm going to need the Phillips.
Kate The who?
Malcolm Phillips screwdriver. It's in the car. I'll get it. Won't be a minute.

Malcolm goes out

The Lights fade on Malcolm and Kate's

Trevor Look, Nick . . .
Nick Yes?
Trevor Something happened tonight you've got to know about.
Nick Yes?
Trevor Jan and I—we met at that party and we—and Susannah came—and we were together and etcetera etcetera and . . . it was nothing at all—nothing to it at all—but I wanted you to be the first to know about it.
Nick Thank you.
Trevor You see, I don't know if you've heard but I've been going through this whole thing—this whole—me and Susannah and well . . .
Nick That's OK, I quite understand.
Trevor You do?
Nick Yes, yes. Of course. See you again soon then.
Trevor Yes.
Nick I'd see you out only I've wrecked my back, you see. I can't get up. Absolute agony.
Trevor Yes. yes. Fine. (*He sits at the dressing-table*)

Cross-fade to Ernest and Delia's. Delia is coming out of the bathroom in her dressing-gown as Ernest returns

Delia Well, where is she?
Ernest Still in the downstairs bathroom.
Delia What on earth is she up to?

Ernest Well, I don't really know. I passed the door just now on my way to the kitchen and I thought I heard voices.

Delia Voices? (*She collects up the pilchard plates*)

Ernest She appears to be talking to someone. Or to herself.

Delia To herself I hope. Unless she's using our downstairs bathroom for secret assignations.

Ernest You never know. She's a very peculiar sort of girl altogether. I hope she isn't going to be much longer. I'd rather like to go to bed.

Delia (*giving the plates to Ernest*) Well, you mount guard down there darling. (*Tidying the bed*) And bring her up when she's finished whatever it is she's doing.

Ernest Right. It's very chilly down there, you know. The Aga's gone out.

Delia Oh Lord.

Ernest goes out

Delia gets into bed and reads a magazine

Cross-fade to Nick and Jan. Jan enters with two mugs of tea

Jan Have you finished talking?

Nick I don't know if he has. I have.

Jan (*giving Nick his tea*) Here. (*Approaching Trevor*) Trevor—Trevor—he's asleep.

Nick He's what?

Jan Ssh.

Nick What do you mean ssh? He can't sleep here. Wake him up. Wake up!

Trevor grunts

Jan Leave him for a minute.

Nick He really is the limit, isn't he? Why doesn't he go home and sleep? Like anyone else.

Jan Because Susannah's probably locked him out. Look, I'll just go and dry my hair. When I've done that, I'll wake him up and pack him off.

Nick He really is the limit

Jan You don't want me to wake him up now, do you? He'll only start talking to you again.

Nick All right, all right. Leave him, leave him ...

Jan He looks so peaceful (*She starts to go, laughing*)

Nick Ha ha.

Jan goes to the bathroom, taking Trevor's mug of tea for herself

Cross-fade to Kate and Malcolm's. Malcolm returns with a screwdriver

Malcolm Here we are. Right. I'm going to take it out on the landing.

Kate Can't you do it in here?

Malcolm It's a surprise. Anyway there's more room out there.

Kate Oh, all right.

Malcolm (*consulting the plan*) Now, where do we start? "Locate panel A which will form the inner side of the drawer unit—figure 1". Panel A? Ah—yes, right—now...

Kate She's very odd isn't she, Susannah? A very odd person.

Malcolm You're right there .... Support bar B. Where's that?

Kate She said something very peculiar to me.

Malcolm B? B? B? Don't tell me they haven't given me a B.

Kate She said she got attracted by other girls in the street.

Malcolm Who said that?

Kate Susannah.

Malcolm I didn't know she was like that.

Kate I don't think she is really.

Malcolm Well, fancy that. Ah-ha. Support bar B.

Kate No, I don't think she's like that. You could tell if she was.

Malcolm Well, it's not normal, is it? For a woman? Fancying girls in the street.

Kate No, but—well...

Malcolm You don't feel like that, do you?

Kate No, but...

Malcolm I didn't think so.

Kate No.

Malcolm Not you. Mrs Normal, that's you.

Kate That doesn't sound very exciting, does it?

Malcolm Suits me. Locking bar C for the second drawer...

Kate You don't think I'm too normal, do you?

Malcolm How can you be too normal?

Kate Well—you see things, you know. And you think, well—I might be missing out on something.

Malcolm How do you mean?

Kate Well...

Malcolm You're happy enough aren't you?

Kate Yes. I just thought that I might be—I could be a more exciting person. Perhaps.

Malcolm (*studying the plan*) You're all right.

Kate But are you excited at all by me, Malcolm?

Malcolm Oh yes. Mad about you ... Where the hell is locking bar C?

Kate No. Seriously.

Malcolm What are you on about?

Kate Well, I looked at those magazines of yours.

Malcolm Magazines? What magazines?

Kate The ones you hid under your socks in the drawer.

Malcolm Oh. You found those did you?

Kate Well, I couldn't help it. I mean, I'm in and out of your sock drawer all day. I mean, I didn't mind...

Malcolm Somebody gave them to me at work. I didn't even read them.

Kate I did.

Malcolm Oh.

Kate No, I just think perhaps I could be more exciting. For you. I'd hate you to get bored.

Malcolm I'm not bored. I'm just trying to find locking bar C.

Kate You will tell me if you get bored with me, won't you?

Malcolm Yes, sure sure.

Kate And I promise to tell you.

Malcolm What?

Kate If I get bored with you.

Malcolm You don't get bored with me, do you?

Kate No. No. (*Pause*) Not often.

Malcolm What, you mean—when we're—in bed? Here?

Kate Not often...

Malcolm Well, that's nice.

Kate Only once or twice.

Malcolm Bored?

Kate No, not bored. You know, it's just I have my mind on other things.

Malcolm You mean, other men.

Kate No. Ordinary things like, shall we have a carpet in the hall or shall we stain the floorboards. That sort of thing. They're all to do with us. In a way.

Malcolm You mean to tell me while I'm—giving my all—you're lying there thinking about floorboards?

Kate Only sometimes.

Malcolm Bloody hell. (*He snatches up some of the pieces*) I'm going in the hall.

Kate Have I hurt your feelings?

Malcolm No. Not at all. I'm just going in the hall.

Malcolm goes out angrily

Kate I just don't want to get boring.

Cross-fade to Ernest and Delia's. Delia is in bed. Susannah comes in cautiously

Susannah Hallo.

Delia Susannah. Come in, dear, how are you? A late visit. (*She rises*)

Susannah Yes. (*She sits on the dressing-table chair*)

Delia We were just—going to bed. I think Ernest is making us some cocoa.

Susannah Oh.

Delia We often have cocoa. Sometimes hot milk but usually cocoa.

Susannah Oh.

A pause

Delia Now. What's the problem? (*She sits on the bed*)

Susannah It's...

Delia Mmm?

Sussanah It's just...

Delia Mmm?

Susannah What am I going to do, Delia?

Delia You're talking about you and Trevor.

Susannah I've lost his respect.

Delia Oh surely not. What makes you think that?

Susannah When he's there deliberately making love to another woman. Knowing...

Delia Trevor was?

Susannah Knowing that I was bound to come in and see them.

Delia Another woman?

Susannah Yes.

Delia Who was this?

Susannah Oh, that woman. Jan...

Delia Jan? Not *the* Jan?

Susannah Do you know her?

Delia Oh yes, yes.

Susannah He's brought her here, has he?

Delia Oh yes, several times. I mean, not since he's been married to you. This was years and years and years and years ago. I mean, he's never looked at another woman. I mean, not since he's been—busy married to you. If there's one thing his father and I always instilled in him from birth it was loyalty. Loyalty to us. Loyalty to the ones he loves. And especially loyalty to the woman he marries.

Susannah He despises me.

Delia Oh, nonsense.

Susannah Do you know what it's like to be ignored?

Delia Well, yes. As a matter of fact I do. We all do. We all get ignored sooner or later. Ernest ignores me dreadfully. I have to tell him everything three times before he'll lift a finger.

Susannah Not only mentally.

Delia Oh. Oh, I see. (*Patting the bed*) It's this old trouble is it?

Susannah Partly.

Delia Oh dear. Dear me. My mother used to say, Delia, if S-E-X ever rears its ugly head, close your eyes before you see the rest of it.

Ernest enters with a tray of three mugs of cocoa

Ernest Cocoa is served.

Delia Oh, well done.

Ernest (*handing Susannah a cup*) Susannah.

Susannah Thank you.

Ernest gives Delia a cup and sits between Delia and Susannah

Ernest Well, now, what are we all chatting about.

Delia Nothing. Nothing that need concern you, dear.

Ernest Oh. On to—those things, are we? Good health.

Susannah We were talking about physical relationships.

Ernest Oh, were you? Jolly good.

Susannah Delia was saying it's probably the cause of all our problems.

Ernest Really?

Delia I said—something like that, yes.

Ernest Did we have any problems? I didn't think we had. I don't think I had any problems. Probably have a problem now but I don't remember having any then. (*He laughs*)

Delia Darling, I wonder if you'd like to slip in to the bathroom for a moment.

Ernest Bathroom?

Delia Just for a moment.

Ernest Oh, all right. (*He rises*)

Susannah You don't have to go.

Delia Yes, I think he does have to. I'd prefer it.

Ernest Right. I'll—be in the bathroom then.

Ernest goes into the bathroom

Delia I'm sorry. I find it rather difficult to talk about this sort of thing in front of Ernest.

Susannah Isn't that—awkward for you?

Delia No, no. We just don't talk about it. We never have talked about it. I think there's far too much talking about it anyway. I mean, I think people would be far happier if they were just left to get on with it.

Susannah But if they have difficulties—hang-ups...

Delia Well, if you have difficulties surely you go to your doctor. Talk to him. They love talking about it. Mine does. In fact, he's got an almost macabre interest in it. For a man of his age.

Susannah I mean, mental problems. That affects how you approach everything. I mean, I am physically afraid of Trevor. He's a very violent, passionate person really and I—I don't think I can be.

Delia Oh dear. That is difficult. Of course, Ernest never was. I spent most of my time trying to get him to notice me at all.

Susannah Can you tell me about it?

Delia About what?

Susannah About—that side of it. With you and your husband.

Delia Don't forget your cocoa.

Susannah No thank you, I—

Delia Don't you want it?

Susannah No, I—

Delia Something else then?

Susannah No, it's—

Delia Tea? Have a cup of tea. I'll make you a cup of tea.

Susannah No, it's—

Delia Nothing like tea. (*She rises and takes Susannah's mug*) Yes, that is a problem for you, isn't it. I don't quite know what we do about that. Wait here. I won't be a moment.

Delia goes out

Cross-fade to Nick and Jan's. Nick is in bed: Trevor still asleep. Jan comes in from the bathroom to fetch her comb

Nick He's starting to snore.

Jan I'll wake him in a minute.
Nick Please do...

Cross-fade to Malcolm and Kate's. Kate is still on the bed. Malcolm enters for another section

Malcolm Why don't you get into bed?
Kate I'm all right.
Malcolm (*rummaging about in his tool-box*) Well, I'll try and be less boring for you in future.
Kate I didn't mean that.
Malcolm Tomorrow night I'll come to bed in a funny hat.
Kate Oh crikey. What have I started.
Malcolm I don't know. And this damn plan's no use, either. (*Very irritably*) One-inch sevens, where are they?
Kate One-inch what?
Malcolm Never mind. Nobody ever told me before I was boring. And I've been with a few, I can tell you.
Kate Yes. I know, you've told me.
Malcolm They weren't bored. None of them were bored. No woman who's been in bed with me has ever complained of boredom. That was the last thing on their mind. If I were you, I'd start worrying that there wasn't something wrong with you.
Kate That's what I am worrying about.
Malcolm You'd do well to. You'd do right to. (*Marching to the door and turning for a parting shot*) Ask Doreen Foster if she was bored with me. She'll tell you.

Malcolm goes out, slamming the door

Cross-fade to Ernest and Delia's. Susannah stands alone

Susannah I am confident in myself. I have confidence in myself. I am not unattractive. I am attractive. People still find me attractive.

During this, Ernest emerges from the bathroom. Seeing her, he attempts to tiptoe across to fetch his book from the bedside table without disturbing her

I am not afraid of people. People are not frightening. There is noth... (*She sees Ernest*)
Ernest (*embarrassed*) Just—fetching a book. Carry on. (*He goes to the door*) *Tom Brown's Schooldays*. Fearfully good. Read it, have you? No? Carry on.

Ernest goes. Susannah wanders slowly out the other way

Cross-fade to Nick and Jan's. Trevor suddenly wakes up

Trevor No, the point is, Nick...
Nick Huh what?

Trevor What? Sorry, did I . . .

Nick You just startled me.

Trevor Have I been asleep?

Nick Yes.

Trevor Sorry.

Nick Quite all right.

Trevor I don't think I was asleep, I was . . . Nick, Nick you're a friend, aren't you? I mean, I know there's Jan and all that—she was mine, now she's yours and you're the luckiest man in the world but—I think I know you. And I trust you.

Nick Thank you.

Trevor And I'd like to know more about you.

Nick Ah.

Trevor And frankly, I'd like you to know more about me. (*Bounding up*) I know, I've got a great idea. Why don't we take a walk? Now? Why not? Come for a walk?

Nick I can't come for a walk, Trevor. I've told you. I have a splintered spine. I'm lying here in agony.

Trevor Oh. Tell me about Jan, then.

Nick Jan? (*He goes back to his book*)

Trevor Jan as she is now. I mean, when you met her, when she came to you from me was she badly destroyed?

Nick No.

Trevor Had I in fact destroyed her?

Nick No, I think she'd forgotten about you completely by the time she met me.

Trevor But you see what I'm driving at, though?

Nick No.

Trevor If I destroyed Jan, maybe I'm destroying Susannah in the same way. Maybe I'm just a destroyer of people.

Nick Now that is possible.

Trevor You think that is possible?

Nick No. Look, Trevor, I don't want to belittle your powers of destruction in any way but it does appear to me that whereas Jan is a perfectly ordinary, normal—reasonably normal—woman—fairly well-balanced—that, in my experience, nothing short of a nuclear charge is likely to destroy—Susannah from our brief acquaintance was born a wreck, is even now a wreck and will probably die one.

Trevor (*taking this in*) You think it's an inherent part of Susannah's character?

Nick Yes.

Trevor Not me at all.

Nick No. I don't think you've helped but . . .

Trevor That's an interesting theory.

Nick Just a thought. I mean, you must have known what you were taking on when you married Susannah.

Trevor She seemed to understand.

Nick Ah well, yes. Most women look as if they understand. Then you find half of them haven't a bloody clue what you're talking about.

Trevor Is that what you find with Jan?

Nick I find the best of Jan is that she's amusing occasionally, very efficient when she wants to be—pretty bright and the worst is that she can be totally self-obsessed, erratic, bad-tempered and unreliable. But taking it all in all, I could have done worse. (*He goes back to his book*)

Trevor I found her a very gentle person.

Nick Really? Well...

Trevor Odd, isn't it? How one person to someone can be something different to someone else? (*He lies on his back on the bed beside Nick. Reflectively*) I remember one day...

Nick What the hell are you doing?

Trevor	I remember this one magic day when Jan and I, we went off together...
Nick	Look, Trevor, you've got your shoes all over the eiderdown.
Trevor	(*casually lifting his feet*) Sorry. We went to the seaside. It was one of those perfect days...
Nick	Look, Trevor...

Speaking together

Jan enters brushing her hair

Jan Oh, that looks cosy. What are you up to?

Nick Look, Jan, will you tell him to get his feet off my eiderdown.

Jan Trevor! Shoes off, please.

Nick Not just his shoes off. Get off altogether. What's he doing lying on my bed anyway?

Jan He's not doing any harm.

Nick He's doing considerable harm. This is my bed. I don't happen to want people sprawling all over it.

Trevor (*getting up*) Sorry. Sorry. I didn't realize.

Nick What nobody in this house seems to realize or appreciate is that I am in considerable physical discomfort. In fact, a great deal of pain. And it is not helped when people sprawl all over the damn bed.

Jan Come on, Trevor. Come and help me wash up.

Trevor Right. Sorry, Nick mate. Sorry.

Jan We'll leave him to it.

Jan goes followed by Trevor

Nick And will somebody remember to remind me that I have to phone Arthur Hewitson tomorrow morning at home.

Jan (*off*) All right, all right.

Nick (*yelling after them*) And don't you two start anything in there. Do you hear me? Do you ... (*He bangs his elbow*) Aaaah. (*He lies back*)

Cross-fade to Malcolm and Kate's. Kate is lying on the bed, wincing at the sound of heavy hammering in the hall. A clatter

Malcolm (*off*) Oh damn and blast this thing.

Kate Malcolm.
Malcolm Damn and blast it.
Kate Malcolm, why don't you come to bed? Leave it till the morning, love.

Malcolm marches in clutching two pieces of splintered wood

Malcolm Look at that. Snapped in half. It was cut half an inch too big. I
   tried to get it in place and what happens it snaps in half. Useless. Useless.
   I'm writing a letter to this lot, I can tell you.
Kate You're very tired—it's nearly three o'clock.
Malcolm I am not tired.
Kate Leave it for now.
Malcolm Oh, no. I'm going to finish it.
Kate Well, can I help at all?
Malcolm No, you cannot. This is a surprise for you. Now go on, get into
   bed. And go to sleep.

Malcolm stamps out

*Kate sadly gets into bed. As if by reflex and without really noticing what she's
doing, she removes a hairbrush, three make-up jars and a couple of hairsprays.
She lies down. The banging starts again in the hall with renewed fury*

*Cross-fade to Ernest and Delia's. Susannah and Delia enter. Susannah with a
cup of tea, Delia with a slice of cake on a sideplate*

Delia (*chatting cheerfully as they come in*) ... no, we had elastic on ours round
   here. We had terrible problems if they got too tight ... Oh, he's still in the
   bathroom. Good. Now, we're going to have to put you somewhere, aren't
   we? And we haven't really got an awful lot of choice. I think you're going
   to have to share with me if you can bear that. Ernest can go in the spare
   room. He won't mind at all.
Susannah Are you sure...?
Delia No trouble. Now, you're positive you're not hungry?
Susannah (*she sits on the bed*) No.
Delia This time of night, I get ravenous. (*She takes a bit of cake*) Now, remember, three simple rules. Feed him properly. Make sure he's clean clothes
   in the morning. And most important of all, don't tell him anything you
   don't have to. A little bit of mystery never did anyone any harm. (*She opens
   a drawer in the dressing-table*) You'll have him eating out of your hand—
   this is delicious for a shop cake. Now, we must find you a nightie. You'll
   have to excuse the smell of pilchards when you first get into bed. You'll
   find it wears off after a little. (*Holding up a nightdress*) Now, how about
   this?
Susannah Thank you.
Delia It's a bit old ... now, what else?

Ernest comes out of the bathroom

Ernest Right. That's it. I don't care what you're talking about I'm not sitting in that bathroom a moment longer. I have now finished *Tom Brown's Schooldays*, there is nothing else in there to read and I'm going to bed.

Delia Yes, we've decided to give you the spare room.

Ernest The what?

Delia The spare room. Trevor's old one. You'll be sleeping in there.

Ernest What, the one with the damp patch, you mean? Not on your life.

Delia Now don't be silly, it hasn't rained for days. Susannah's staying the night and she's sleeping with me in here.

Ernest In here?

Delia Yes.

Ernest In my bed.

Delia Just for the night. I'll come and help you make up the bed in there. Oh, and you'll probably need a bottle. You deal with the bottle. The bathroom's just through there, Susannah. Use anything you find.

Susannah goes out. Delia goes out

Ernest (*following*) I don't think I've ever spent a night like this in my life.

Ernest goes

Cross-fade to Nick and Jan's. Trevor comes in with a tea-towel to fetch Nick's dirty cup. Jan appears in the doorway. Trevor indicates Nick

Jan (*sotto*) Is he asleep?

Trevor (*sotto*) Yes.

Jan Good. He's been absolutely foul all day.

Trevor Has he?

Jan He can't bear it if he's in bed. Absolutely loathes it. He's so bad-tempered you would not believe it. I've got to put up with this for days.

Trevor Oh.

Jan Imagine that all day long. Count yourself lucky you've only got Susannah. She can't be worse than him at the moment.

Nick I am not asleep. I heard that.

Jan Good.

Nick Is he going home now?

Jan No, he's sleeping here.

Nick Who said so?

Jan I did. Want to argue? He's sleeping on the sofa. Come on, Trevor.

Trevor Oh. Can I ring Kate first? She's waiting up for me, you see.

Jan Oh, they'll have gone to bed by now.

Trevor No, she said she'd wait up. I'll just give her a quick ring.

Jan If you like. I'll get the number. I've got it somewhere.

Nick Make sure he pays for the call.

Jan Ignore him. (*Heading to the door*) I'm sure they'll have gone to bed, you know.

Jan goes

Trevor (*following her out*) I'd feel better if I phoned.

Trevor goes

Cross-fade to Malcolm and Kate's. Banging from the hall

Malcolm (*off*) Get in, you bastard, get in will you. (*More banging*) Get in ... (*More banging and a final crash*)

Malcolm staggers in, bleary and dishevelled

Kate Have you done it?
Malcolm Give me a hand in with it, will you?
Kate (*jumping out of bed and following him off*) Oh, right, I'm dying to see it.

Malcolm and Kate carry on the dressing-table. It is a lopsided mess. They set it down. Kate steps back

Kate Oh. Yes ... yes ...
Malcolm Well, it's—not quite right but ...
Kate It's very nice. I like the drawers. (*She pulls one out. It is stuck*)
Malcolm Hang on, hang on, don't force it. (*He pulls at the drawer without effect. He tugs at it. He wrestles with it and finally delivers it a mighty blow with the flat of his hand. The drawer opens*) I'll ease them a little in the morning.
Kate It's very handsome.
Malcolm Not bad.
Kate I'm just a bit worried things might roll off the end.
Malcolm Roll off the end?
Kate With it being a bit on the slant.
Malcolm Well, it's got to be finished off. It's got to be sanded down yet.
Kate Oh, I see. Well. Well done.
Malcolm Most of their stuff didn't make sense. I had to make half this up as I went along.
Kate That's not right is it? Are you coming to bed now?
Malcolm (*squinting at his masterpiece*) Yes, yes. Just a sec.
Kate It's very late.
Malcolm You hop in. I'll join you.
Kate (*getting into bed*) Don't be long.
Malcolm No. All I need to do, you see, is to sand down the feet at this end a bit. It's only a matter of a—of a little bit. (*He lifts the thing on to its side*) Just a moment.
Kate What are you doing now?
Malcolm Won't be a moment.

The phone rings

Who the hell can that be?

Kate answers the phone. Lights up on Nick and Jan's to reveal Trevor at the other end

Kate Hallo?
Trevor Hallo. Kate?
Kate Yes.
Trevor It's Trevor.
Kate Oh, hallo Trevor. (*To Malcolm, sotto, covering the receiver*) It's Trevor.
(*Into the phone*) Where are you, Trevor?
Trevor Look, I hope it's all right, I'm staying over with Nick and Jan here.
Kate Oh, I see. I have made the bed up.
Trevor Yes well, thanks all the same, Kate. So just to say don't wait up.
Kate No, right, I won't. I won't. Thank you for phoning, Trevor.
Trevor Yes, well. Good night then, Kate.
Kate Good night, Trevor.

Trevor rings off and goes out

(*Replacing the receiver*) He's not coming back after all.
Malcolm Good. Now then, let's have a look at this. (*He takes out a selection of sandpapers from his tool-box and sifts through them*)

Cross-fade to Ernest and Delia's. Delia enters followed by Ernest. She takes his pillow from the bed and hands it to him

Delia Now, you'll be perfectly comfy in there. I don't know what you're complaining about.
Ernest I shall probably finish up with marsh fever.
Delia Nonsense. (*She tidies the bed*)
Ernest On your head be it. That's all I can say ... (*He breaks off*)

Susannah's voice is heard from the bathroom repeating her "exercises". They both go to the door to listen. It opens

Susannah emerges

As she does so, Ernest and Delia scatter, Delia to continue tidying the bed, Ernest, after a quick glance at Susannah in her nightie, to the hall

Ernest goes

Delia Oh, that suits you.
Susannah Thank you.
Delia Much nicer than on me. Do you mind sleeping that side?
Susannah No, no.
Delia (*taking off her dressing-gown and slippers*) We tend to lie in a little on Sundays so don't feel you have to get up. Actually, Ernest usually makes a cup of tea for me, so maybe we'll be lucky. Right, everything you want?
Susannah (*getting into bed*) Fine.
Delia (*doing likewise*) Now, if I do happen to dig you with my elbows—Ernest often complains I do that—just push me out of the way. Don't worry, you won't wake me.
Susannah Right.

Susannah takes Delia's pillow just as Delia lies back to put her head on it. Delia bounces up again, and looks at Susannah

Delia Lights out, then.

Delia turns out her bedlamp. Susannah does the same

Delia Sleep tight.
Susannah Good night.
Delia Sweet dreams.

Cross-fade to Nick and Jan's. Jan enters ready for bed, with a glass of water and two tablets

Jan Well, that's Trevor settled. It makes quite a nice bed that sofa.
Nick Oh good. Now perhaps you can wrench your attention round to me.
Jan Glass of water. (*She hands it to him*)
Nick What for?
Jan Two of these. (*She hands him two tablets*)
Nick They are absolutely...
Jan Come on. Come on, please. I want to get to bed.
Nick Oh.

He takes the pills. Jan gets into bed

Are we sleeping with the light on?
Jan Just for a second. I want to think.
Nick Can't you think in the dark? I mean, I thought I was supposed to get rest. This place has been like a major trunk road.
Jan In a minute.
Nick (*after a slight pause*) It beats me what you ever saw in that man.
Jan Trevor?
Nick Yes. I mean, it doesn't say much for me. I mean, if he was your first choice that makes me your second choice.
Jan I like a contrast. Shut up, I'm thinking.
Nick Was he...
Jan Mm?
Nick Was he—you know. Good?
Jan Good?
Nick In bed.
Jan Why do men always want to know that? I mean, how am I possibly expected to answer that?
Nick Truthfully.
Jan If I say yes, he was marvellous, you'll sulk, won't you? Whereas if I say no, awful, you'll just lie there looking smug all night.
Nick Not at all.
Jan (*after a pause*) Well, I'll say this. He thinks he's awfully good.

Nick laughs

That satisfy you?
Nick Thank you. Thank you.
Jan Oh, look at him. Just look at him. Why didn't I keep my mouth shut.

Jan switches off the light

Cross-fade to Ernest and Delia's. Delia and Susannah are in bed asleep. Susannah is making weird moaning noises. She starts to flail about. Delia wakes up. She looks alarmed. Susannah's wails increase in volume. She begins to claw and clutch at Delia. Delia fends her off

Delia Oh lord. Oh lord. Susannah. Susannah.

Delia switches on the light

Susannah (*sitting bolt upright awake*) Wah—wah...
Delia It's all right, dear. You're all right. Just a nasty dream.

Ernest comes in

Ernest Anything wrong? I heard shouting.
Delia Susannah had a little dream. That's all dear. Nothing serious.
Ernest Oh. Did she? Did she? For your information, there is steam rising off my top blanket in there. Thought you might like to know. Good night.

Ernest goes out

Delia Better now, dear?
Susannah (*who has lain down again half asleep already*) Mmm.
Delia Good night.

Delia switches off the light again. A slight pause. Susannah starts again

Susannah No—no—no ... No—no—no ... No—no—please—no—no ...
Delia Oh heavens...

Cross-fade to Malcolm and Kate's. Kate is invisible under the sheets. Malcolm is on the floor and has fallen asleep in the midst of sandpapering. He snores

Cross-fade to Jan and Nick's

Nick (*restless unable to get to sleep*) Oooh—ow ... (*Softly*) Jan? Jan? Are you asleep? Jan? ... Ooh—ow. (*Loudly*) Aaah.
Jan (*waking up*) What?
Nick Sorry. Did I wake you? It's just agony.
Jan Well, try and sleep darling.
Nick Impossible, I'm afraid.
Jan Well, do try...

Jan turns over. Nick lies, moaning to himself softly

Cross-fade to Ernest and Delia's. Susannah is now quiet. Delia sleeps sedately. Susannah suddenly sits bolt upright, her eyes wide open

Susannah Ooooooaaaah! Trevor...
Delia (*awake in a flash*) What? What?
Susannah (*fumbling her way out of bed*) I must phone Trevor.
Delia (*switching on her light*) Not now, dear. It's only a quarter to seven.

Susannah Please, please I want to phone Trevor.

Delia Well, there's a phone here. Don't go out there, you'll wake Ernest. And if you wake Ernest before he's ready, he gets very tetchy. Here we are.

Susannah I'll just phone home. (*She dials*)

Delia It's far too early to telephone anyone. Far too early . . .

Susannah It's ringing.

Delia And Trevor hates being woken up early. I could never get him to school on time. He's worse than Ernest.

Susannah There's no reply.

Delia He'll be dead to the world. Try again later on. Now go back to sleep . . .

Susannah No, no, he would have heard. I know he would have heard. I had this terrible dream . . . I'll see if he's still at Malcolm's. (*She goes to her handbag*)

Delia No. Now you really mustn't. It's very naughty of you. Phoning people up at this time of the morning. I absolutely forbid it.

Susannah But I'm worried to death about him. Don't you see? Don't you care?

Delia (*quietening her*) Yes, yes, all right, all right.

Susannah (*scrabbling for her address book in her bag*) Malcolm and Kate . . .

Delia You're going to be dreadfully unpopular . . .

Susannah (*dialling*) I'll ask Kate if she knows where he went. He may still be there.

Delia I hope you don't carry on like this at home. You can never hope to keep a husband if you keep bobbing up and down like this all night.

Lights up on Malcolm and Kate's. The phone rings. Malcolm remains asleep. Kate's head emerges

Kate Ooooo—aaah—oh . . . (*Answering*) Ho. Hoo hiss.

Susannah Kate?

Kate Hes.

Susannah It's Susannah.

Kate Oh. Ho.

Susannah I hope I haven't woken you.

Kate Ho. Ho.

Susannah Is Trevor there?

Kate No . . . no, he's not. He went to Jan's. Night night. (*She hangs up and slumps back*)

Lights down on Malcolm and Kate's

Susannah (*thunderstruck*) He's at Jan's.

Delia What?

Susannah (*beginning to crumple*) I knew it. I knew he would be. He's at Jan's.

Delia Now, Susannah.

Susannah I dreamt he was at Jan's.

Delia Now come along, pull yourself together.

Susannah He's gone back to Jan. I knew he'd go back to Jan. (*She flings herself on the bed weeping hysterically*)

Delia Now, Susannah. Susannah. I shall smack your face. Susannah.

Ernest enters angrily, putting on his dressing-gown

Ernest Look, what the blazes are you two playing at? Banging and thumping and wailing. It's like sleeping next door to a girls' dormitory.

Delia Ernest dear...

Ernest It's too bad, you know. Too bad. I just this minute got off to sleep against considerable odds. (*He puts on his spectacles*)

Delia Ernest, we have a crisis.

Ernest I know we have a crisis. And if I don't get my sleep, there's going to be a bigger one.

Delia Ernest, please. Quietly, darling. Quietly. Please...

Ernest What?

Delia You're going to have to do something. Will you do something please? Then we can all get some sleep.

Ernest Anything.

Delia Right. Will you pick up that phone, please. And ring Jan whatever-her-name-is and ask to speak to Trevor. And then you can put him on to me.

Ernest Why should I want to ring Jan?

Delia Because that apparently is where Trevor is.

Ernest At this time of the morning?

Delia Especially at this time of the morning.

Ernest Oh, no. You don't mean to say...

Delia Apparently.

Ernest Oh, no. Well, I warn you, I'm not in any mood for pleasantries. Give me the number then. (*He lifts the receiver*)

Delia Susannah.

Susannah Mm?

Delia What is Jan's number? (*Holding up the address book*) Will it be in here?

Susannah (*nodding mutely*) Mmm.

Delia Where do I find it? What's her husband's surname?

Susannah Davies.

Delia Davies. (*Handing the book to Ernest*) Look up Davies, dear, under D.

Ernest (*searching*) Davies? Davies? Davies? Nick and Jan Davies. Those the ones?

Delia That's them.

Ernest Two six—um—um—seven four—(*dialling*)—two—six ...

Delia Ask to speak to Trevor.

Ernest I shall.

Lights up on Nick and Jan's. The phone rings

Nick (*waking up and trying to sit up*) Aaah. (*He lies back*)

Jan (*asleep*) Phone's ringing.

Nick Well, answer it darling. Will you come round and answer it.

Jan (*stumbling out of bed*) Oh no.

Nick Oh my God, it's probably America. Lights on.

Jan What?

Nick Lights on.

Jan Right. (*She switches on the light*)

Nick Notebook, quick. Pen and notebook. Come along, darling. Quickly please, they'll hang up.

Jan Pen and notebook.

Nick Jan please, get a move on.

Jan I am getting a move on. (*She answers the phone*) Hallo? Two six ...

Ernest Hallo. Is that Jan?

Jan Yes, just a moment please. I'll give you my husband.

Ernest I don't want your husband, young lady. I want to speak to my son.

Jan Your son?

Ernest I know he's there. Come along.

Jan Oh I'm sorry. I thought you were America. Just a second ... (*To Nick*) It's not America. It's your father.

Nick My father? Good Lord. (*Taking the receiver*) Hallo there, Dad.

Ernest Hallo, who's that?

Nick It's Nick, Dad, how are you? When did you get back?

Ernest Back?

Nick I thought you were in Rome.

Ernest Rome?

Nick Who is this?

Ernest That's not Trevor.

Delia Who are you talking to?

Ernest Haven't the foggiest. Some fellow who thinks I'm in Rome.

Nick Look, did you say Trevor?

Ernest Yes. Trevor. I'm talking to Trevor. We seem to have a crossed line...

Delia Oh, give that to me. (*She takes the receiver*)

Ernest Bloody GPO. Absolutely the last straw.

Delia (*ultra-charming*) Hallo, who am I speaking to?

Nick Madam, you are speaking to a man with a bad back in considerable pain. More to the point, who are you?

Delia I'm so sorry to disturb you. This is Trevor's mother speaking.

Nick You want to speak to Trevor, do you?

Delia If it's not too much trouble. Thank you so much.

Nick (*handing the receiver to Jan*) Trevor's mother. It runs in the family.

Jan Delia?

Delia (*to Ernest*) There, that's that sorted out.

Jan Hallo, Delia. It's Jan. Do you want a word with Trevor?

Delia Yes, is he with you, Jan?

Jan Yes, he's sleeping on the sofa. I'll get him.

Jan goes

Delia Thank you, Jan. She is a nice girl. Her husband sounds a very grumpy thing.

Ernest I'm not surprised.

Delia Now then. She's obviously with her husband, Susannah, so there's nothing at all for you to worry about. She's just fetching Trevor. He's sleeping on their sofa apparently.

Trevor blunders in. He has been sleeping in his shirt, pants and socks

Nick Could you not use the phone in there?
Trevor Sorry to disturb you.

Jan enters, speaking

Jan No, Trevor, I said you can take it in here, Trevor.
Trevor (*answering the phone*) Hallo.
Jan Trev ... (*apologetically to Nick*) Sorry. (*She gets into bed*)
Trevor Hallo.
Delia Trevor?
Trevor Hallo, Mum.
Delia I have Susannah here, Trevor. She wants to talk to you.
Trevor Oh. Right.
Delia (*holding out the phone*) Susannah.
Susannah Thank you. (*Into the phone*) Hallo—Trevor? (*She kneels on the floor*)
Delia Ernest. (*She waves him away*)

Ernest stamps back into his room

Trevor Hallo, Suse.
Susannah I thought I'd ring you.
Trevor Yes.
Susannah To say. I'm sorry. About this evening...
Trevor No. It was me. I'm sorry. (*He walks up and down by the bed*)
Susannah Well.
Trevor Yes, well.
Susannah Yes. (*She lies on the floor*) Trevor, I think we ought to try again.

Jan and Nick look at Trevor

Delia (*softly*) Aaaah.
Trevor Yes. Yes. OK.
Susannah Are you alone?

Trevor looks at Nick and Jan, who retire beneath the clothes

Trevor Not really.
Susannah Is she with you?
Trevor Yes. Yes.
Susannah Are you still keen on her?
Trevor No. No.
Nick Is this going on for long?
Trevor Nick's here too, Suse. He's in bed. (*To Nick*) Could you say hallo to Susannah to prove you're here? (*He sticks the receiver under the bedclothes*)
Nick I'm not saying hallo to anyone at this time of the morning.
Trevor Thanks. Did you hear that, Susannah?
Susannah Yes.

Trevor Well. I'm sleeping on the sofa.
Susannah Oh.
Trevor Where are you sleeping?
Susannah With your mother.
Trevor Oh.
Susannah Look, I could be home in ten minutes. I've got the car.
Trevor Well. OK. So could I.
Susannah Shall we do that?
Trevor Sure. Fine.
Susannah OK. See you then.
Trevor Yes. Sure. 'Bye.
Susannah 'Bye-bye.
Trevor 'Bye.

Susannah and Trevor hang up. Susannah rises

Delia Well, everything settled?
Susannah (*hurrying to the bathroom*) I'm going to get dressed. Excuse me.

Susannah goes

Delia Dressed?
Trevor (*to Nick*) Thanks a lot. Thanks a lot.
Nick Want to phone anyone else while you're here?
Trevor No, no. That's fine, thanks. I'll be off home then. I'll just get dressed. Thanks, Jan.
Jan All right, Trevor.

Trevor goes out

Nick I'm going to get my firm to sue that man. He's set me back about a month.
Jan Try not to be quite so unplesant. (*She kisses him*)
Nick Ow.
Jan Sorry, sorry. Back to sleep now. (*She turns out the light*)

Susannah returns from the bathroom struggling into her clothes

Susannah Trevor says he's going home. (*She packs up her belongings*) So I'm going home too. Thank you for everything.
Delia Quite all right. Would you like a hairbrush before you go.
Susannah Hairbrush? Oh, all right. (*She picks up a clothes-brush and gives her hair a couple of quick strokes*)
Delia You ought to do a little something with yourself. For Trevor's sake.
Susannah All right.

Susannah rushes off

Back at Nick and Jan's, Trevor comes in

Trevor I say. I say...
Nick Oh no...
Trevor I'm off.
Jan All right, Trevor. 'Bye-bye.
Trevor I say...
Jan Yes..
Trevor I wonder if I could make a quick phone call?
Jan Phone call?
Trevor Would you mind? I can't get the one in there to work.
Jan No, you have to switch it through.
Trevor Switch it through?
Jan Never mind. Use this one.
Trevor Are you sure?
Nick (*screaming*) Look, take the phone! Take it!
Trevor Thanks. Just a quick one.
Jan I'll put the light on.
Trevor No, it's all right. I can see. I can see.

Trevor goes to the phone table. He fumbles about. A clatter

Nick Aaaah! Aaaaah!
Trevor Sorry.
Jan What...? (*She switches on the light*)

Trevor has knocked Nick's glass of water on to the bed

Nick You bloody fool.
Trevor Sorry, sorry, sorry.
Jan (*getting out of bed and going out*) All right, all right. Hold on, hold on.

Jan goes

Trevor Sorry. (*He dials*) I should get up and pull the sheet over this way a
bit if I were you.
Nick (*yelling*) I can't get up! For the last time, I can't get up! You idiot.
Trevor Sorry.

The phone rings in Delia's bedroom

Delia (*answering*) Hallo.
Trevor Hallo, Mum. It's Trevor again.
Delia Trevor. Oh—you want Susannah. She's just gone. Hold on, I'll see if
I can catch her ... (*Running to the door and shouting*) Susannah! Susannah!
Susannah (*very distant*) Yes.
Delia Telephone. (*She hurries back to the phone*) She is just coming, Trevor.
You just caught her.

*Jan enters and starts to mop up Nick, slipping off his pyjama jacket and pulling
the sheet sideways from under him so that he no longer lies on the damp patch.
She puts the pyjama jacket over Trevor's arm. Meanwhile at Delia's, Ernest
enters hurriedly*

Ernest All right, all right, I'm coming. Who is it?
Delia No, darling, not for you. For Susannah.
Ernest Oh my God.

Susannah bursts past Ernest

Susannah Excuse me.
Delia Trevor again for you, dear.
Susannah (*taking the phone*) Hallo, Trevor. I was just leaving.
Trevor Look, Suse, I was just thinking. I think I'd better just clear things up first.
Susannah How do you mean?
Trevor Well, I was thinking—Malcolm and Kate. I mean, we ruined their party last night.
Susannah Yes, I know.
Trevor Well. They're good friends. I don't want them to think—well—that I'm not sorry. I think I have to go round and see them.
Susannah It's a bit early, isn't it?
Trevor Oh no, Malcolm's always up at the crack of dawn. He won't mind, don't worry. Anyway. So could you meet me there? Then we could drive home.
Susannah All right. Malcolm and Kate's.
Trevor OK. See you then.
Susannah Right. 'Bye.

They hang up

Thank you. Good-bye. Good-bye, Ernest.
Ernest Good-bye.

Susannah rushes out

Ernest sits on the bed

Trevor Well. See you then. (*He puts the pyjama jacket on top of Nick*)
Jan Yes.
Trevor 'Bye, Nick. 'Bye.

Trevor goes out

Jan Right. You comfortable now?

Nick utters a low moan. The Lights fade out on Nick and Jan

Ernest I'm sorry. I am firmly of the opinion that that girl is completely potty. Not only potty but dangerously potty.
Delia No, she's not really. She's quite sweet. Very, very, very dim—but quite sweet natured.
Ernest Am I to be allowed back into my own bed?
Delia Yes, it's all yours.

Ernest You haven't got any more people dropping in?
Delia Not as far as I know.

They get into bed

Ernest Well, once I'm in, I'm not getting out again.
Delia Not if you don't want to.
Ernest And I'll tell you something else. If you want your morning tea...
Delia Yes?
Ernest You're going to have to whistle for it.

Cross-fade to Nick and Jan's. Nick moans

Jan What is it?
Nick (*feverishly*) Jan—promise me. Don't let him back in here again. Please
  don't let him back in here again. Never let that man back in here again.
Jan (*concerned*) All right, darling, all right. I won't ... (*She strokes his brow*)
Nick Please, promise me.
Jan (*soothingly*) Yes, yes.

*Cross-fade to Malcolm and Kate's. Kate is under the bedclothes. Malcolm is
still asleep on the floor. The front doorbell rings. It rings again*

Kate Mmmmm...
Malcolm (*wakening*) Uh. Oooh...
Kate Malcolm.
Malcolm Oooh.
Kate (*emerging*) Malcolm? What are you doing?
Malcolm I must have fallen asleep.
Kate Was that a bell?
Malcolm Was it?

The doorbell rings

Kate Front door.
Malcolm All right, I'll go ... (*He tries to get up*) Har—I've got cramp.
  Cramp—cramp—cramp.
Kate Right. Don't worry ... (*She slides out of bed, still in her dressing-gown*)
  I'll go. Walk around a bit.

  Kate goes downstairs

Malcolm Walk around a bit.

*Malcolm manages to stand. His head lists over to one side. He seems unable
to straighten it. The arm on which he has slept hangs uselessly. One of his legs
seems reluctant to support him*

  Kate returns cautiously

Kate Malcolm.
Malcolm Uh?
Kate Malcolm, it's Trevor.

Malcolm Who?
Kate Trevor.
Malcolm Trevor. (*He stands*)

Trevor enters

Trevor Hallo, Malcolm mate. Oh, you're dressed. I'm glad I didn't get you up.
Malcolm (*bemused*) What are you doing here?
Trevor Malcolm—Kate, look. Look...
Malcolm What is he doing here?
Trevor I've come to say sorry.
Malcolm What are you doing here?
Trevor I realize that last night—unforgivable. I—sorry. Sue and I, we're very, well, you know...
Malcolm Ah.
Kate Thank you, Trevor.
Trevor So.
Malcolm Yes. Cheerio then.
Trevor Yes.

A pause

Kate (*moving to the door*) Well...

Trevor starts to follow her, then returns

Trevor Er—do you think I could just hang on for a couple of seconds? I arranged to meet Susannah here, you see.
Malcolm Here?
Trevor Yes.
Malcolm Ah.
Kate Malcolm, would you like a bath?
Malcolm Bath?
Kate It'll loosen you up. You look very tense.
Malcolm All right. Yes. All right.
Kate I'll run it for you.
Malcolm No. I'll do it. I'll do it. You keep an eye on him.
Kate All right.

Malcolm limps lopsidedly out

Well...
Trevor We're really genuinely sorry, Kate. We're both going to try to...
Kate Yes...
Trevor If we possibly can.
Kate Yes.

An awkward pause

Look what Malcolm made last night. (*She indicates the masterpiece*)

Trevor Ah yes.
Kate Out of a kit. He had a bit of trouble with it. It's got to be sanded yet.
Trevor Yes.
Kate You can see it's a bit down at one end.
Trevor Ah yes.
Kate And the drawers are a bit stiff. But he's going to ease those.

They survey it

Trevor You could maybe just—get it more even if you did this with it—like this.

He takes the top and tries to bend it to one side. The top comes away in his hand. Unsupported, the entire thing drops to pieces

Trevor Ah.
Kate (*appalled*) Oh no. Oh no.
Malcolm (*off*) What's going on?
Kate Nothing, dear, nothing. Have your bath. Oh Trevor, what have you done?
Trevor Sorry.

The doorbell rings

I could maybe get it together again for you. It doesn't look as if...
Kate No, don't touch it, Trevor. Don't touch it at all. I'll just tell him it—suddenly collapsed. Wait there.

Kate goes

Trevor examines the wreckage

Kate returns with Susannah

Here she is.
Susannah (*shyly*) Hallo.
Trevor Hallo.
Kate (*aware of being in the way*) I'll just see if Malcolm's managing.

Kate goes

Trevor Look, Suse—this may not work but—I'm going to try, you know. I'm really going to try.
Susannah Well. I'm going to try. That's all we can do really.
Trevor You see, I think if we could just...
Susannah Communicate...
Trevor Yes...
Susannah Yes. (*She sits on the bed*)
Trevor (*sitting next to her*) Well, we're on the bed again.
Susannah (*embarrassed*) Yes. It's a start.
Trevor Yes. I'll try not to rush you, Suse. I think I really rushed you.
Susannah Well. Maybe a bit.

Trevor My fault.
Susannah No, my fault.

He strokes her hair awkwardly. She clings to him

Trevor You cold? You're shivering.
Susannah A little bit. Tired. I think...
Trevor (*drawing the blanket round her*) Well. I think we both are. Been a busy night.
Susannah Yes. (*She kicks off her shoes and tucks up by him*) We shouldn't do this.
Trevor Just for a second. He's having a bath.
Susannah (*contentedly*) Mmm. This is nice. (*She slides her feet down under the covers*) Ow.
Trevor What?
Susannah Something in the bed. (*She produces a saucepan*) What's this doing in here?
Trevor I don't know.
Susannah They have all sorts of things in their bed. I found boots in the pillow-case.
Trevor (*knowingly*) Ah well. People get up to strange things, you know. Some people...
Susannah Yes.

Trevor cuddles up to her. She holds his head in her arms

I've been thinking. We must do something about our house. I think that's important. I want to start trying to make it more of a home. I—haven't been very good at that. I mean, somewhere nice ... then you'll want to come home all the more, won't you? And I'll try and cook. I mean, really cook ... and make sure you have some clean clothes in the morning and ... well. You know what I mean, don't you? Trevor? Trevor ...?

Trevor is asleep

(*Alone*) Oh ... I am confident in myself. I have confidence in myself. I am not unattractive. I am attractive. People still find me attractive. I am not afraid of people. People are not frightening. There is nothing to be frightened off...

As Susannah speaks the Lights fade slowly, and—

the CURTAIN *falls*

FURNITURE AND PROPERTY LIST

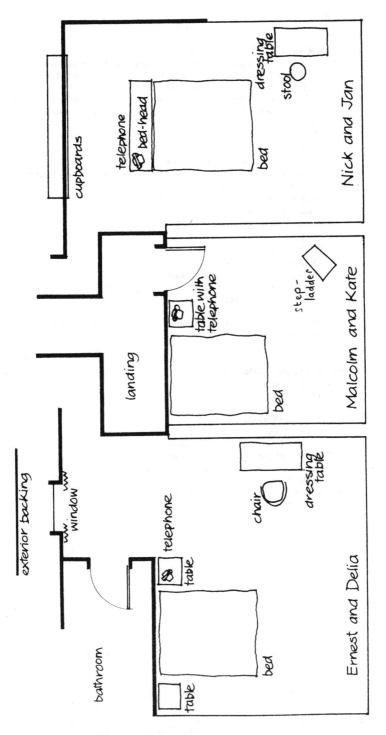

ACT I

On stage: ERNEST AND DELIA'S ROOM:
　　Double bed and bedding: **Ernest's** pyjamas, **Delia's** nightdress
　　2 bedside tables. *On them:* 2 bedside lamps, telephone, box of tissues, copy
　　　of *Tom Brown's Schooldays*, clock, magazine
　　Dressing-table. *On it:* brushes, combs, general make-up items, clothes-
　　　brush, **Delia's** handbag. *In drawer:* nightdress, other clothing
　　Chair
　　Window
　　Carpet

　　MALCOLM AND KATE'S ROOM:
　　Double bed and bedding (unmade). *Hidden in it:* hairbrush, 2 hair-sprays,
　　　3 make-up jars, saucepan
　　Bedside table. *On it:* telephone, bedlamp
　　Small stepladder
　　On floor: large cardboard package
　　Carpet

　　NICK AND JAN'S ROOM:
　　Double bed and bedding
　　Bedhead. *On it:* telephone, bedlamp
　　Dressing-table. *On it:* brushes, combs, general make-up items, necklace,
　　　earrings, hair-dryer
　　Stool
　　Wall cupboards. *In them:* various articles of clothing, including jacket
　　On floor near bed: book
　　Rugs

Off stage: Kate's shoes (**Malcolm, Kate**)
　　Shirt (**Malcolm**)
　　Towel (**Kate**)
　　Aerosol shaving soap (**Malcolm**)
　　2 drinks (**Malcolm**)
　　Several piles of coats (**Malcolm**)
　　Plate of Cornish pasties (**Malcolm**)
　　2 plates of pilchards on toast (**Ernest**)
　　Tool-box, including sandpapers (**Malcolm**)
　　Towel (**Jan**)
Personal　**Ernest:** watch, keys, change, spectacles
　　Jan: watch

ACT II

Strike: Cardboard package
Set: Pieces of easy-to-assemble dressing-table on floor in **Malcolm** and **Kate's**
        room, with wrapping paper and plan
        Malcolm's tools scattered on floor
Off stage: 2 mugs of tea (**Jan**)
        Screwdriver (**Malcolm**)
        Tray with 3 mugs of cocoa (**Ernest**)
        2 pieces of splintered wood (**Malcolm**)
        Cup of tea (**Susannah**)
        Slice of cake on side plate (**Delia**)
        Tea-towel (**Trevor**)
        Lopsided dressing-table, made to collapse (**Malcolm** and **Kate**)
        Glass of water and 2 tablets (**Jan**)

LIGHTING PLOT

Property fittings required: 4 bedlamps (2 for **Ernest** and **Delia,** 1 for **Malcolm** and **Kate,** 1 for **Nick** and **Jan**)

Interior. 3 bedrooms. The same scene throughout

EFFECTS PLOT

ACT I

ACT II

MADE AND PRINTED IN GREAT BRITAIN BY
LATIMER TREND & COMPANY LTD PLYMOUTH